THIS IS THE
SIAMESE CAT

The famous FAN-T-CEE'S TEE CEE, an example of excellent head type, ears, and eye slant.

by
MARGE NAPLES

Published by T.F.H. Publications, Inc., T.F.H. Building, 245 Cornelison Avenue, Jersey City, N. J. 07302. Distributed in the British Empire by T.F.H. Publications (London) Ltd., 13 Nutley Lane, Reigate, Surrey, England. In Canada by Clarke, Irwin & Company Ltd., Clarwin House, 791 St. Clair Avenue West, Toronto 10, Ontario, Canada. Printed in the U.S.A. by the lithograph process by T.F.H. Lithograph Corp., Jersey City, N. J. 07302.

Distributed to the Book Trade in the U.S.A. by Crown Publishers, Inc., 419 Park Avenue South, New York, N. Y. 10016.

Dedicated to
LaVona Wright, a dear friend, who started me in the Cat Fancy with Siamese Cats.

ACKNOWLEDGEMENTS

I wish to extend sincere thanks to my many friends for the use of the photographs of their cats.

I want to offer very special thanks to Jeanne Ramsdale for her continued encouragement and invaluable help, and to Philip Ramsdale, D.V.M., who volunteered to check the chapter on illnesses of our cats.

A most sincere "thank you" goes to my photographer, Victor Baldwin, who offered many of the illustrative photographs taken of his own cats and kittens.

Louise Van der Meid was the official photographer.

© 1964 *by T.F.H. Publications, Inc.*
Rights reserved throughout the world.

CONTENTS

INTRODUCTION 6
CHAPTER I—HISTORY OF THE SIAMESE CAT 7
  Some Fables . . . Some Facts
**CHAPTER II—THE SHOW STANDARD FOR
    SIAMESE CATS** 10
  Head . . . Ears . . . Eye Shape . . . Eye Color . . . Body Type . . . Neck . . . Tail . . . Legs and Feet . . . Coat . . . Body Color . . . Points . . . Condition . . . Colors of Siamese . . . A Brief History of Albino Siamese
**CHAPTER III—CHARACTERISTICS OF THE
    SIAMESE CAT** 24
  Reputation . . . Environment . . . Personalities . . . The Siamese Voice . . . Understanding Your Cat . . . Different Colors Differ in Personality . . . Curiosity and Climbing . . . Watch Cats . . . Sneaky Siamese Cats? . . . A Study in Ears . . . Siamese With "Seams" and "Stitching" . . . An Active Cat . . . A Sad Note
CHAPTER IV—HOW TO BUY A SIAMESE KITTEN 44
  Buy a Good Kitten . . . How to Find a Kitten . . . What to Look for in a Kitten . . . What You Should Expect to Pay . . . Male or Female? . . . Why Alter Your Pet? . . . Don't Let Your Siamese Run Loose . . . Two Kittens? . . . A Suggestion . . . What Color? . . . Teach Children to Care for Their Pets
**CHAPTER V—CHOOSING HIS NAME AND
    REGISTERING YOUR KITTEN** 58
  Pet Names . . . Use of Cattery Names . . . Length of Name Limited . . . Thai (Siamese) Words With English Translations . . . Registering Your Kitten . . . Which Association?
CHAPTER VI—TRAINING YOUR KITTEN 66
  Be Gentle But Firm . . . Training to Stay Indoors . . . Loose Cat! . . . Training to a Leash . . . Scratching and Exercise Posts . . . Teach Your Kitten to Retrieve . . . Toys . . . Training to a Litter Box . . . Training to Use the Toilet . . . The Bathtub . . . Train to a Whistle . . . Train to Sit Up . . . Car and Boat Training . . . Vacationing With Your Cat . . . Carriers . . . Shipping Your Cat . . . Introduction to a New Home . . . A Safe Home? . . . Sleeping Habits . . . Wool-Eating Cats . . . Cats and Asthma . . . Dress Up Your Cat . . . Cat Clothes for People

CHAPTER VII—GROOMING 113
   Coat ... Bathing ... Claws ... Ears ... Eyes ... Teeth
   ... Fleas ... De-Clawing
CHAPTER VIII—FEEDING CATS AND KITTENS 123
   Kittens ... Vitamins ... A Diet for Siamese ... Milk ...
   Water ... Food From Your Table ... Quantity of Food
   ... How to Feed ... What Not to Feed
CHAPTER IX—HEALTH OF YOUR KITTENS
   AND CATS 135
   Veterinarian ... Is Your Cat Sick? ... How to Give a Pill
   or Capsule ... How to Give Liquid Medication ... How
   to Take a Cat's Temperature ... Diarrhea ... Constipation
   ... Poisons ... Ringworm ... Maggots ... Eczema ...
   Bites ... Teeth ... Cystitis ... Anemia ... Aspirin ...
   Simple Cold ... Convulsions ... Parasites ... Viral
   Diseases and Vaccinations ... Hairballs ... Gingivitis—
   Sore Gums ... Stud Tail
CHAPTER X—CATTERIES 180
   Evolution of a Cattery ... The Ideal Cattery ... A Cage
   for One Cat? ... A Novel Idea ... Cleanliness ... The
   Dispensary ... Registration of Your Cattery ... Income
   Taxes
CHAPTER XI—STUD CATS AND QUEENS 187
   Young Males ... Spraying ... Stud Cats ... To Locate a
   Stud ... Stud Fee ... The Visiting Queen ... Heat, Season,
   or Calling ... Cats Differ From Other Animals ... Double
   Mating ... Unplanned Matings ... They Do Have to
   Learn
CHAPTER XII—MOTHERHOOD AND KITTENS 197
   When to Expect the Kittens ... Symptoms of Pregnancy
   ... Feeding the Mother Cat ... Eclampsia ... Miscarriage
   ... As Delivery Nears ... The Day of Birth Arrives ...
   The Uterus ... Breech Birth ... The Sac and Placenta
   (Afterbirth) ... Removing the Sac ... Severing the Cord
   ... Removing Fluid From Lungs ... Stimulating Circula-
   tion ... The Placenta (Afterbirth) ... Are There More?
   ... Fix a Dry Nest ... Get Acquainted With Your New
   Family ... Delivery on Two Different Days ... Premature
   Kittens ... Care of Premature, Weak, or Orphan Kittens
   ... Abnormalities ... Euthanasia (Painless Destruction)
   ... If Your Queen Is in Trouble ... The Kitten a Mother
   Ignores ... Care of The Kittens ... Drying Up a Mother
   Cat's Milk

CHAPTER XIII—BREEDING 214
  Breeding Goal . . . Inbreeding — Line Breeding — Out-Crossing . . . Color Breeding
CHAPTER XIV—CAT ASSOCIATIONS AND CLUBS 217
  Cat Fanciers' Association . . . How to Join a Club . . . A Few Interesting Facts
CHAPTER XV—SHOWS 220
  How to Obtain an Entry . . . Entry Blanks . . . Cost of Putting on a Show . . . Getting Ready for the Show . . . Cage Decorations . . . A List of Things to Take Along . . . Show Time . . . Leaving the Cat Overnight . . . Show Etiquette . . . The Show Circuit . . . Agenting Cats . . . Jungle Cats on Display
CHAPTER XVI—SHOW COMPETITION AND
    NATIONAL SCORING SYSTEMS 228
  Show Competition . . . National Scoring Systems
SIAMESE LORE 236
INDEX 237

INTRODUCTION

THE WISDOM OF CATS vs. THE STUPIDITY OF MAN

When cats fight, they fight as individuals, driven by the storms and stresses of nature, in whose soul there is always conflict. They do not march in serried lines, like an exceptionally stupid breed of sheep, to the command of a cackle from a radio.

Legions of Tabbies do not suddenly advance across Yellowbrook Bridge in order to destroy legions of Siamese lined up on the opposite bank, merely because some pampered Persian whom none of them has ever met has ordered them to do so. Well, they don't, do they? Yet this is precisely what men do.

Battalions of White Cats from the East End do not suddenly lose their reason, band together, and charge up Main Street in order to battle to the death with opposing battalions of Black Cats from the West End, merely because some cat in the suburbs, who was probably a dingy shade of brown, anyway, has thought up some idiotic slogan about the Supremacy of the White (or Black) Cats. Yet that too is precisely what men do.

And so let's pick for our subject the Siamese Cat.

All cats have many similarities, but to those of us who choose to live and share our lives with Siamese, they are the ultimate in domesticated felines. Siamese are much more than just ordinary cats. Their intelligence is almost unbelievable. We can learn many things from them. Personally, I feel my life has been vastly enriched since we acquired our first Siamese cat, enriched by the cats themselves, by persons I have met through selling and in the Cat Fancy, and by the intriguing experiences encountered while showing our cats.

CHAPTER I

HISTORY OF THE SIAMESE CAT

After exhaustive research for a true history of this strikingly beautiful breed of cat, I am convinced that records simply were not kept on their origin. No one doubts that they originated in Siam (now Thailand), but further than that their history is lost in fable and fantasy.

It is said that Siamese cats were sacred in Siam, and were owned only by the King and members of the royal family. If, as is believed, these cats were used as temple guards, it must have been very impressive to approach a temple and see panther-like cats just daring anyone to intrude.

The customary dress of the fine ladies of the Court was a high headdress of many precious jewels, choker-type necklaces, rings on their fingers and toes, and bracelets on their arms and legs. Even the leashes for their cats were jewel-encrusted. The Siamese cats of this time probably were much larger than those of today, and they no doubt were predominantly Seal Point in color.

In almost every book about Siamese cats, we are told different fables of the reasons for their crossed eyes and kinked tails. Regardless of their origin, to this day these two traits have not been entirely bred out of the Siamese.

Some Fables

One fable tells of a Buddhist monk who lived in one of the sacred temples where a golden goblet, once used by the Great Buddha, was kept. The monk took to imbibing of the sacred spirits and sometimes would disappear for many days, leaving just his pair of Siamese cats to guard the temple and the goblet. Once he was gone for such a long time that the two Siamese finally decided that their old friend would not return and that another monk must be found for the temple. The male Siamese started out on a long journey in search of a new master. He was gone a very long time, but the female cat, left alone to guard the sacred goblet, never left her watch. She stared and squinted at the goblet for so many days and nights that her eyes became crossed and remained so the rest of her life. She became so tired from her long vigil that at last she fell into a deep sleep from sheer exhaustion. However, before she fell asleep, she wound her tail around the goblet, knowing that if anything touched her sensitive tail it would awaken her. Finally, the father Siamese returned with a new monk for the temple. He found the mother cat lying beside the goblet with their family of kittens, all of which had kinked tails and crossed eyes!

Another tale relates how a forgetful Buddhist monk once tied a knot in his cat's tail as a reminder, and it is said that Siamese cats have had kinked tails ever since.

There is another story which tells of a princess's rings being placed on the tail of a Siamese cat and the tail knotted at the end to keep the rings from sliding off; so, of course, Siamese tails were kinked ever after.

The hunters in Thailand today tell us that the Siamese cats there now are very wild, that they are three times as large as the Siamese cats we know, and that there are four colors of the wild Siamese. The reason the breed has been preserved in their wild state is that they will breed only to their own kind—in fact, they kill any other kind of cat they encounter, including the spotted jungle cats.

SOME FACTS

Early records show that the first Siamese cats were imported into England in 1884 by Mr. Owen Gould, British Consul-General, who upon going to pay his farewell call on the King of Siam was given a pair to take home with him. *Cats Magazine* gives 1890 as the date the first Siamese cat arrived in the United States.

In a series of articles by Carlon Boren in the Cat Fanciers Association Year Books in recent years, we are told that a Seal Point male named Madison California, owned by Mrs. Lucy C. Johnstone, was the first Siamese cat in America to win a Championship. The same articles credit Lockehaven Siam, a Seal Point male imported from France, owned by Mrs. W. E. Colburn of Chicago, with being the first Siamese to win Best Cat in Show. This win was at the Michigan Cat Club Show in Detroit, Michigan, in 1907.

The first Siamese, and the only Shorthair, to win the Cat of the Year award given by *Cats Magazine* was a Blue Point male, Triple Grand Champion Tempurra's Yours Truly, in 1956. This cat, owned by Mr. and Mrs. Richard Birkett of San Francisco, was then retired from competition. He was sired by the famous Ta-Lee-Ho's Al-La-Bi. Tempurra's Yours Truly was insured by Lloyds of London for $1,500.

Several Siamese have won the Opposite Sex Cat of The Year award in the competition scored by *Cats Magazine*. They are:

1947—Double Champion Vee Roi's Lantara Gene, Blue Point Female,
      owned by Mrs. R. H. Hecht

Blue Point female owned by Noel and Helen Arthur, bred by Harriet Wolfgang: QUAD. GR. AND SEXTUPLE CH. WOLFGANG LIEBSTI II OF THANI, 1962 OPPOSITE SEX CAT OF THE YEAR. Sire: Tr. Gr. Ch. Fan-T-Cee's Phoenix of Wolfgang; dam: Marhan Mingene Wolfgang. Photo by John H. White.

1948—Double Champion Vee Roi's Katisha, Seal Point Female, owned by Mrs. R. H. Hecht

1950—Grand Champion Vee Roi's Lantara Gene, owned by Mrs. R. H. Hecht

1952—Grand and Double Champion Cymri Dee-Va, Seal Point Female, owned by Lillian Pedulla

1954—Grand Champion Ammon Ra's Taisho, Seal Point Female, owned by Lillian Magner

1958—Grand Champion Wolfgang's Melody of Be-Ba, Seal Point Female, owned by Mr. and Mrs. E. T. Baker

1962—Quadruple Grand and Sextuple Champion Wolfgang Liebsti II of Thani, Blue Point Female, owned by Noel and Helen Arthur

CHAPTER II

THE SHOW STANDARD FOR SIAMESE CATS

The show standard will acquaint you with the several colors of Siamese cats, and with the different things to look for.

The following is incorporated from The Siamese Standard of five National Cat Associations (see Chapter XIV).

SCALE OF POINTS

COLOR	25
Body—Shadings, tone and depth of color	
Point color—Depth, evenness, conformation to pattern	
COAT	10
Closeness—shortness	
CONDITION	5
TYPE	20
Body, Neck, Tail, Legs, Feet	
HEAD	20
Profile, wedge, chin	
EYES	20
Shape, color	
TOTAL	100

HEAD

The head should be long and well proportioned. It should narrow in perfectly straight lines to a fine muzzle. Viewed from the front, a wedge should be created by straight lines from the outer ear bases along the sides of the muzzle, without a break in the jaw line at the whiskers. The skull should be flat, and the nose should be a continuation of the forehead, with no break. The profile should be a straight line, without a dip, as seen from the center of the forehead to the tip of the nose and from the tip of the nose to the chin. Allowance is to be made for jowls in stud cats.

Blue Point female owned and bred by Mr. and Mrs. Howard Krebs: DBL. GRAND & TRIPLE CH. KREBS FLAMBEAU. Sire: Krebs Don Juan; dam: Fan-T-Cee's Electra of Krebs. Photo by Victor Baldwin.

Objections:
 Round or broad head, short or broad muzzle, bulging forehead, receding chin or overshot chin (meaning that the teeth of the lower jaw do not meet those of the upper jaw, coming either behind or in front of them. The teeth of both jaws should meet). Roman nose. (A hump in the nose is known as a Roman nose.)

EARS

The ears should be erect, rather large, wide at the base, and pricked forward as though the cat is listening. There should be the width of an ear between the ears. The ears should continue the line of the wedge.

Objections:

Small or short ears. Improper ear set. Too wide or too narrow between the ears.

Seal Point male owned and bred by Mrs. Fred Galvin: DBL. GR. AND QUINT CH. FAN-T-CEE'S TEE CEE. Sire: Kabar's Calypso; dam: Kabar's Miss Fancy of Fan-T-Cee. Photo by Victor Baldwin.

Blue Point male owned by Dr. Francis Coddington, bred by Elsie Quinn: DBL. GR. AND QUINT. CH. QUINN'S BLUE NITE. Sire: Fan-T-Cee's Tee Cee; dam: Mandarin's Destiny of Quinn. Photo by Victor Baldwin.

EYE SHAPE

The eye aperture should be almond shaped, with an oriental slant toward the nose. There should be the width of an eye between the eyes.

Objections:
Round, or unslanted eye aperture. Crossed eyes.

EYE COLOR

Eyes should be clear, brilliant, deep blue in color.

Objections:
Any tinge of green. Pale.

Seal Point male owned by Mrs. Margorie Elliott, bred by Mrs. Fred Galvin: GR. AND TR. CH. FAN-T-CEE'S FANDANGO OF SHAN LING. Sire: Fan-T-Cee's Kabar Kenny; dam: Fan-T-Cee's Enchantress. Photo by "Muzzie."'

Seal Point male owned by Mrs. O. H. Bridge, bred by Mrs. Adolph Olson. MEDICINE LAKE TEX-ZANEE. Sire: Medicine Lake Wee Zano; dam: Medicine Lake Wee Sal.

BODY TYPE
The body should be medium in size, long, lithe, and svelte. Overall body structure should be fine-boned and firmly muscled. Stretched out, the body should resemble a tube. There should be no bulge around the rib cage.
Objections:
A body that is cobby, short, thick, fat, or soft.
NECK
The neck should be long and slender.
Objections:
Short or thick neck.
TAIL
The tail should be narrow at the base, long and tapering. It should not have a visible kink.
Objections:
Short or thick tail, visible kink, evidence of shaved fur.

LEGS AND FEET

Legs should be proportionately slim and long enough to carry the body length gracefully. The hind legs should be slightly higher than the front legs. Feet should be small and oval in shape.

Objections:

Short legs, heavy leg bones. Large or round feet.

COAT

The coat should be very short, fine in texture, glossy, and close-lying.

Objections:

Rough, shaggy or coarse coat. A thick, or heavy, coat, which is referred to as "plush."

BODY COLOR

The body color should be even, with slightly darker shading across the shoulders and back, shading gradually into a lighter color on stomach and chest. Darker coloring should be allowed for older cats. Kittens should be lighter in color generally.

Objections:

Uneven body color or shading. Dark spots on stomach. Tabby or ticked markings. Hip spots.

Lilac Point female owned and bred by Mrs. Helen C. Koscak: GRAND & QUAD. CH. KOSCAK'S FROSTIE LILLI MARLANE. Sire: Koscak's Lu-E-Tu; dam: Koscak's Choco-Vixen. Photo by "Muzzie."

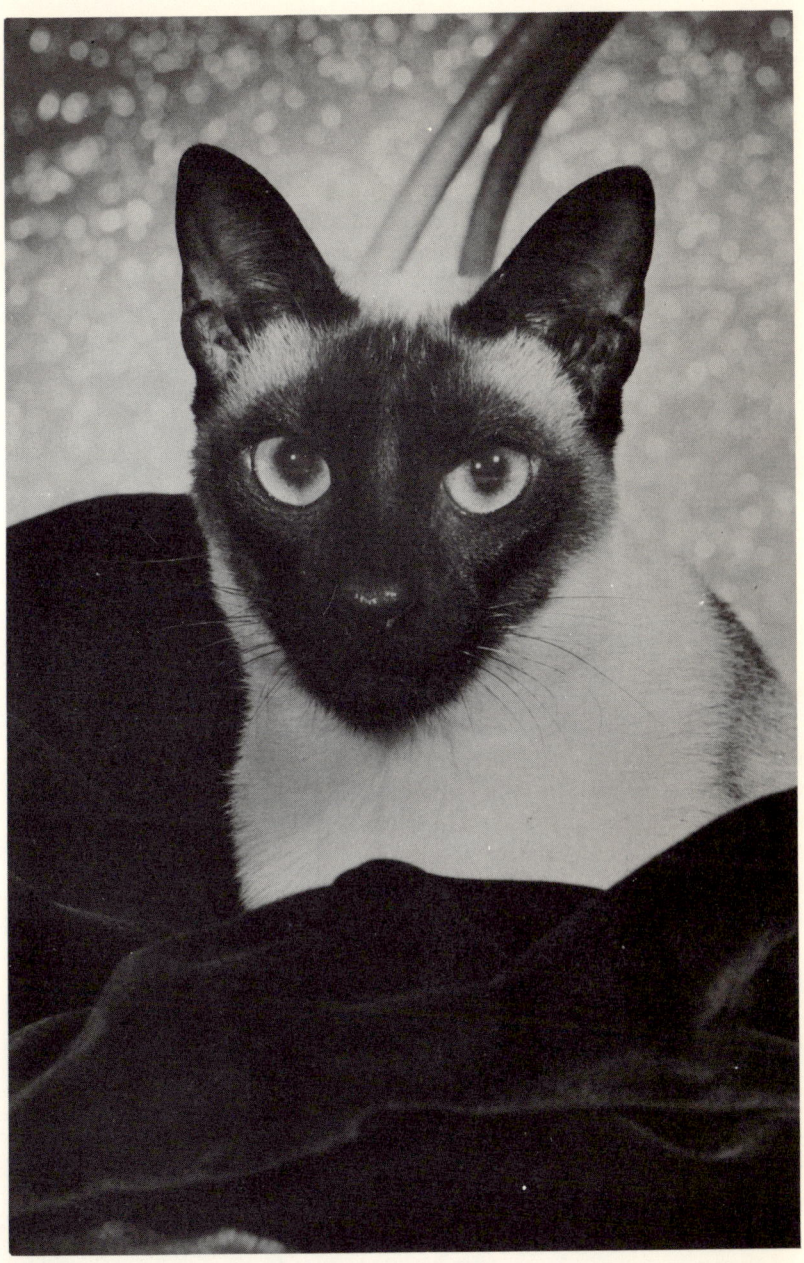

Seal Point female owned and bred by Hazel and Hank Ludkey: R.M. GR. AND QUINT. CH. RENDARA'S FARO QUEEN. Sire: Rendara's Lucky Buck; dam: Rendara's Falena. Photo by Victor Baldwin.

POINTS

The mask, ears, legs, feet, and tail should be clearly defined. Except in kittens, the mask and ears should be connected by tracings. All points should be of the same intensity of color.

Objections:

Complete hood. If the color of the mask continues to fill in and covers the entire head, including part of the neck, it is called a "hood." Light hairs in the points, called "ticking." Bars on the tail or legs. Bars are allowed for in judging kittens.

CONDITION

Hard and muscular, with no indication of fat.

Objections:

Emaciation; flabby, soft muscle tone, also referred to as "mushy."

COLORS OF SIAMESE

Seal Points

The body color of a Seal Point Siamese should be an even pale fawn or cream, shading gradually into a lighter color on the stomach and chest. Points should be a dense, deep seal brown, almost black. All points should be of the same shade. Paw and nose leather should be black.

Objections:

Black or gray shading on the body.

Chocolate Points

The body color of a Chocolate Point Siamese should be an ivory color all over, shading, if at all, to be in the color of the points. The points should be a warm, milk chocolate, as even in color as possible. The ears should not be darker than the other points. As a result of diluted pigmentation of the points, the flesh tones show through the nose leather, resulting in a brownish red tone, while the foot pads should be a tannish pink.

Objections:

Shading on the body. Nose and paw leather dark in tone, like that of a Seal Point, shall be cause for disqualification for competition in the Chocolate Point class in shows.

Blue Points

The body color of a Blue Point Siamese should be a sparkling bluish white, shading, if at all, to be the same gray-blue tone as the points, but of a lighter shade. Points should be a good dark blue of a cold tone, clearly defined, and the color of all points should be of as nearly the same tone as possible. Paw and nose leather to be dark, almost black.

Objections:

Fawn or cream-colored shadings on the body.

Blue Point male owned and bred by Marjorie Fountain: R.M. GR. & CH. FONTAINBLEU BERTIE. Sire: Kreb's Jason of Fontainbleu; dam: Penny's Chai Lai Nin.

Blue Point male owned and bred by Vivian Wheaton: DBL. CH. MALOJA'S MERLIN. Sire: Fran-T-Cee's Kabar Kenny; dam: DiNapoli's Tang-A-Bi Blu. Photo by Erik Wheaton.

Chocolate Point female owned by Mr. & Mrs. Leigh Manley, bred by Mrs. Rex Naugle: DBL. GR. AND QUINT. CH. GREEN LANE BERYL. Sire: Green Lane Van; dam: Green Lane Malvana. Photo by Victor Baldwin.

Lilac, or Frost, Points

Cat Associations (listed in Chapter XIV) differ in the name they apply to this coloration. Some refer to it as Frost Point, others as Lilac Point. The body color of these cats should be glacial white. The points should be a very light silvery blue. There is a slight rosiness to the points, especially the ears, as a result of the blood showing through the very light pigment. The ears, legs, mask, paws, and tail to be as even in color as possible at maturity. No tannish color in any of the points. The pads on the bottom of the feet are of a pinkish coloration. The nose is a translucent dull pink or rose tone (blood tone, actually) showing through the grayed nose.

Objections:

    Tannish color in any of the points or coat.

Red Points or Red Colorpoints

The body color should be a creamy white, with shadings, if any, of dilute red, the same tone as the points. The points should be red, the deeper the shade the better. Since red is a slow-developing, rather reduced color pigment, two years should be allowed for full color intensity to evolve in the points. Kittens should be white, with deeper cream-colored points. This color is not yet recognized by all Associations. One Association permits these cats to be judged with the other Siamese classes; in others, they are judged as a separate breed called Red Colorpoints, since this color actually has been developed by very careful breeding from the Domestic Red cat crossed with Siamese.

Objections:

    Too large, non-Siamese type.

Albino Siamese male owned by Mr. and Mrs. A. G. Holmes: CH. SNOW PRINCE FELIX OF ANARTS. Sire: Count Pierre; dam: Mateka. Photo by George F. Gee Studio.

Any Other Color Colorpoints

This classification includes Tortiepoint Siamese and Blue-Creampoint Siamese. These colors are obtained when developing the Red Point (or Red Colorpoint) Siamese. The color of points should be dense and deep, with all points matching. Body color should be a clear white, with shading, when present, to be the same tone as the points. They should have clearly defined spots of the various colors, all colors on each point, a blaze on the face, and shading in all tones of the points.

Albinos

Albino Siamese should be of a solid white color, with no color whatever in the points. Their eyes should be clear pink, with blue showing through.

Objections:

Any shading or other color in the coat (not permissible). Pale, milky, gray, green, yellowish or dark blue tinge in the eye color.

A Brief History of Albino Siamese

There are comparatively few of these cats. The first recorded were two that appeared in a litter born October 5, 1947, from registered Seal Point parents owned by Lilly A. Burton, of Fontana, California. These two Albinos were sired by Roden's Sun Ling and their dam was Babi Kiti. Not much more was heard of Albino Siamese until recent years. I understand they may be registered in all Associations. Their white coat coloring is not a chalky, dull color, but has the true Siamese sheen and is typically short and close-lying. The pink of the eye color is not that of the albino rabbit, but has a light blue undertone.

CHAPTER III
CHARACTERISTICS OF THE SIAMESE CAT

The Siamese cat combines the grace of the panther, the fleetness of the deer, the softness of down, the strength of the tiger, the affection of the dog, and the courage of the lion. Siamese cats are very beautiful. To have one, or several, of these exquisite creatures sharing your home is a joy indeed. You who love cats have a bit of the artist in your soul, and a Siamese appeals to that side of your nature especially, because they are a continual study in symmetry, grace, and elegance.

Playfulness and sprightly energy characterize kittens of all types, and these qualities are especially evident in fun-loving Siamese kittens. Photo by Louise Van der Meid.

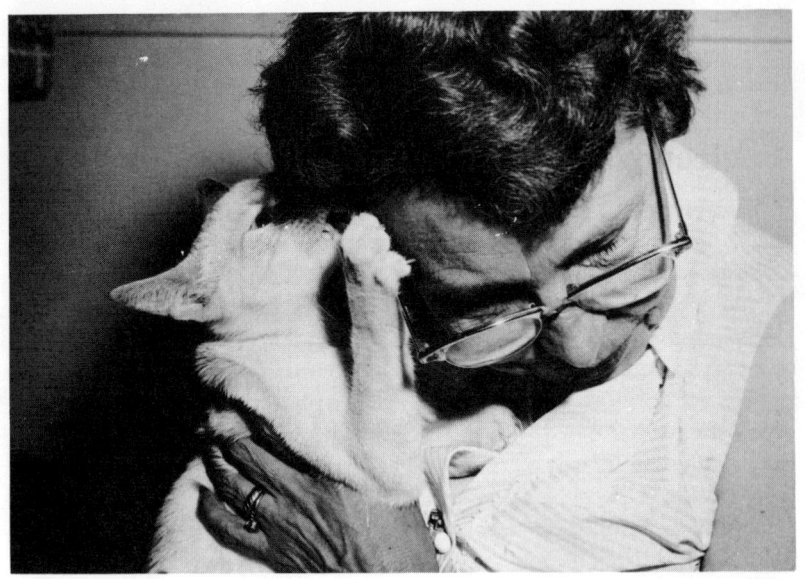

One of the most charming aspects of the Siamese is the way that it displays its affection for its owner; here it seems almost as if this young Siamese is telling a secret. Photo by Louise Van der Meid.

Reputation

The reputation of the Siamese is varied. Too many people are of the opinion that Siamese do not make amiable pets. Nothing could be farther from the truth. True, there is an occasional ill-tempered Siamese, but I believe these exceptions have, somewhere along the line, been mistreated (perhaps the result of owners' lack of understanding their nature), which has made them ill-tempered. The reputation of a few such cats spreads far and wide. The Siamese disposition is not so very different from that of any other cat. You will find a few cats in any breed that are not fond of people. Likewise, you will find quite a few persons who are not fond of cats. Try a Siamese for yourself; if the cat is given half a chance, you could not wish for a finer pet.

Siamese have a decidedly independent nature. They can never be trained with harsh words or any form of unkind treatment. Their understanding comes from their high degree of intelligence. In response to kindness they become devoted pets. They seem to understand exactly what your feelings are and what you want from them, but this is not to say they will always do exactly what you want them to do. They learn very rapidly. If you will take a little time to teach them, you'll find they soon will be doing many tricks. They are natural retrievers. They will entertain both themselves and you for many hours with their antics. You will find yourself watching them in preference to a television program—and your friends will visit so they can watch, too!

Environment

Environment is very important in raising Siamese. In the world of humans, noisy parents usually have unruly children; hence, if you want a loving companion, don't quarrel with your Siamese. These cats are very sensitive. If you are high-strung or nervous, shield your Siamese from your nervous outbreaks as much as possible, as cats tend to reflect the personality of their owners. Take the time to figure out why he is doing something he knows he should not do. With a little imagination, it isn't too difficult. If you hear him using the furniture or rug to sharpen his claws, whereas he usually uses his scratching post, he may be trying to get your attention, and possibly is asking you to leave your chores and play with him. Give him credit for intelligence. You will be astonished at the things he does, and why, if you pause to question and think for a moment.

Blue Point male owned by Mr. and Mrs. Walter J. Weiss, bred by Mrs. Fred Galvin: R.M. TR. GR. AND QUINT. CH. FAN-T-CEE FIRE FLY OF DAZZLING. Sire: Kabar's Alexander the Great; dam: Fan-T-Cee's Blue Fancy.

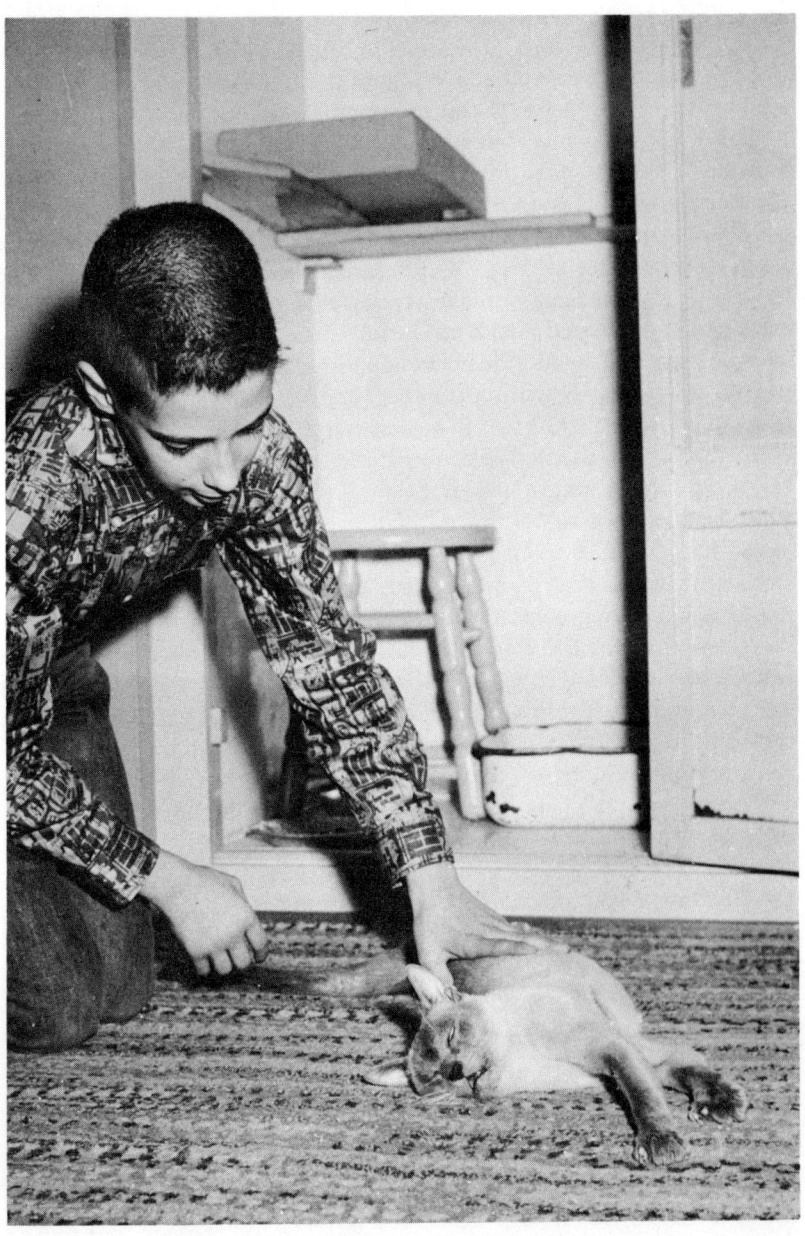
Children enjoy and are benefited by the mutual affection of a child-cat relationship. Photo by Louise Van der Meid.

Personalities

A Siamese cat loves you and is always trying to show you that he does. He likes to play and tease. If you will take the time and effort to understand him, he will constantly amaze you with his ingenuity. All Siamese are individuals, yet in many ways they are very similar. For instance, most Siamese like to drink water from a faucet rather than from a dish set down on the floor for them. Most Siamese do not particularly care for milk. One trait shows up when they are playing and chasing each other at a dead run. The leading cat will suddenly, without warning of any kind, flip over on his back, catching his pursuer off guard, and a make-believe fight will ensue. Kittens, when playing, will "puff" themselves up. That is to say, their fur will stand straight up, especially that on the back, and the tail will resemble a bottle brush. They arch their backs and hop around stiff-legged, circling each other.

Another never-ending delight to the watcher is when one cat succeeds in surprising another: one or both of them will suddenly jump straight up in the air and come down all bristled to immediately start a circling, stiff-legged, "crow hop" type of fencing. Another thing cats do when one challenges another, if the incident doesn't explode into a fight, is after a long time of standing and glaring at each other, with only an occasional low growl, one cat will become tired of the contest and will very slowly start to stalk off in studied slow motion. He will appear to be looking in another direction, but will keep his adversary in sight from the corner of his eye until he is what he considers a safe distance away. If a quick backward glance shows the adversary not in pursuit, he will then go on about his separate business.

Whether you have one Siamese or many, they love to be in your lap whenever you are sitting. If you are working around the house, they will follow you from room to room and curl up, preferably on a piece of clothing, and sleep until you go into another part of the house—unless, of course, you are making a bed. Bed-making will immediately start a hide-and-seek game. This can be exasperating, but much more often it is fun. I usually end up by making the bed up with at least one cat in it!

Of course you know that if you are reading a cat absolutely has to help you. It is almost uncanny how a cat knows exactly what paragraph of a page you are reading, and, if the paper or magazine is lying on a table, he will sit exactly on that spot and stare at you lovingly.

I hope none of you ever condemns a cat for being a cat and trying to catch a bird. Cats have evolved only so far from the wild state, and they attach no sentiment to animal life. The killing of a bird is no more an evil act to a cat than your buying a chicken at the local market is an evil act to you. Nevertheless, even if your cat does not realize that the killing of birds is considered reprehensible—you should, and you should take steps to prevent it.

If your cat brings you an object and lays it on your doorstep, he is bringing you a gift. Remember that he loves you and wants to please you. He thinks a mouse, lizard, or whatever is a great prize, and he wants you to have it. Pet and praise him, and dispose of the "gift" when he can't see you. Imagine how crushed he will be if you scold him and immediately throw away his offering.

It requires intelligence on your part to understand your Siamese. Remember that he will soon learn anything you take the time and patience to teach him. Therefore, when he is young, teach him the way you want him to be as an adult. If you let him jump up on you and climb up to your shoulder when he is a kitten, naturally he will jump from the floor to your shoulder in one easy leap when he is grown. He may also do the same thing to your guests, startling them, to say the least.

If you permit your cat to sleep with you, don't be angry with him when he tries various ways of waking you in the morning. He is hungry. It doesn't occur to him that he is being annoying. Personally, I am thankful for this trait. I'd never make it to work without my fur-covered alarm clock, because I turn off the alarm in my sleep and go right on sleeping more soundly than before. My cat, however, does not give up. If everything else fails, he nips me on the chin!

Siamese are very active, playful, and full of fun as long as they live and feel

Unless a cat is broken of the habit of climbing to your shoulder while it is a kitten it will continue its climbing antics in later life. Photo by Louise Van der Meid.

well, unless you let them get too fat. They are mischievous, humorous, entertaining, and alert. Sometimes people ask if Siamese are related to monkeys. I find it very hard to keep from saying, "Yes, they are a cross between a monkey and a dog," which, of course, is not true at all. However, the description fits almost perfectly.

Chocolate Point male bred and owned by Mrs. Fredric Hokin: GR. & QUAD. CH. DARK GAUNTLETS SIR VIVOR. Sire: Sir Cobalt of the Dark Gauntlets; dam: Wah-Lee-Nang Tu Dark Gauntlets. Photo by Hans Bomskow.

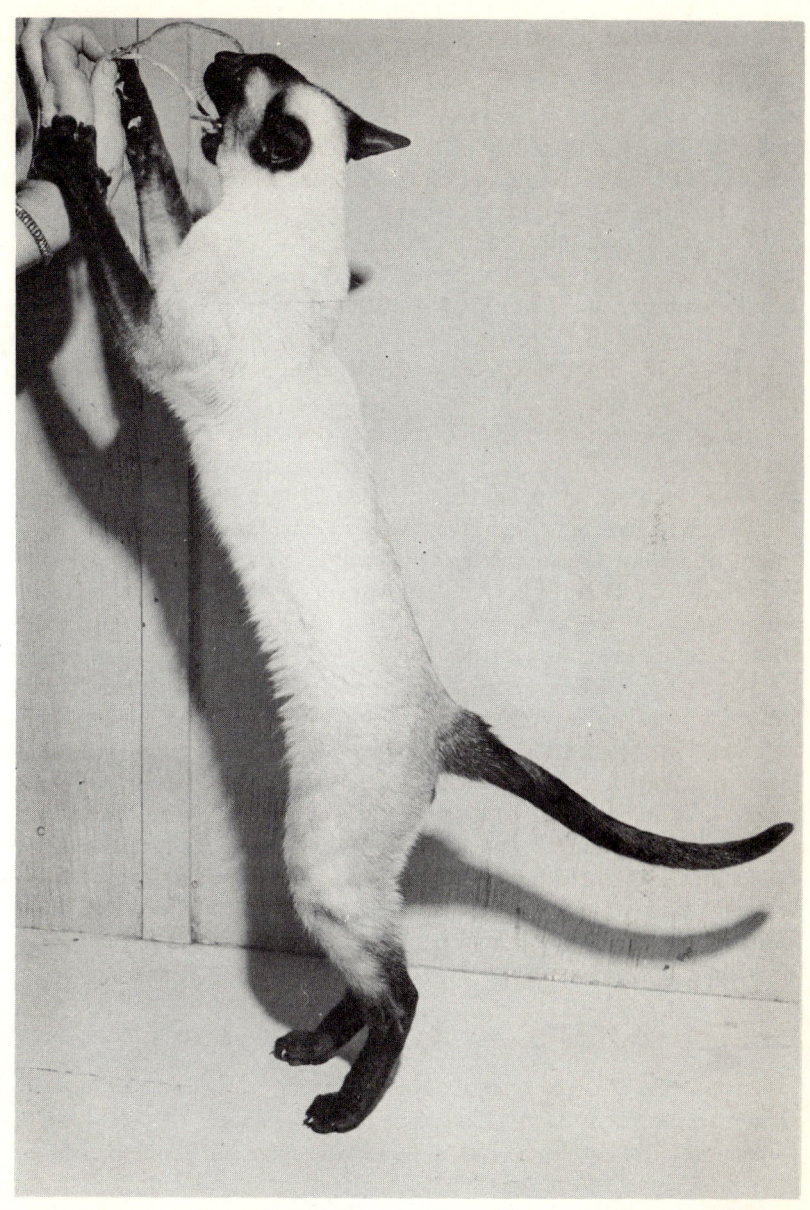

Seal Point male owned and bred by Esther E. Illingworth: CH. DEMBI'S CHUNG WUN. Sire: Dembi's Du-Kee Luv; dam: Dembi's Mei-Lo-Ki. Photo by Jeff Wiener.

The Siamese Voice

Siamese are noted for their voice. Those of us who have lived with them feel their voice is one of the most fascinating things about them.* You can understand your cat infinitely better if you learn to listen to him talking to you. He will usually answer you when you speak to him. Don't be surprised if you find yourself carrying on a conversation with him. Our Blue Tango says "ouch" so distinctly when we take him for a shot that our veterinarian tells everyone about our "talking" cat. This cat has the most expressive voice I have ever heard. It is resonant and it ranges from a soft inquiring tone to an irritated roar. At cat shows I can distinguish his voice above the din, from the opposite end of the hall, and I can tell whether he is just trying to impress everybody or is fighting mad.

Cats often try to convey their messages through pantomime. A cat entwining himself between your ankles is reminding you he is there, he is hungry, or he wants you to hold him. If you walk by your Siamese and he sees you looking at him, often he will lay his head down and then fall over on his side. This means "Please stop and play with me."

Siamese, and all cats, I suppose, talk to each other. It is not too difficult to understand and translate what a stud cat is saying to a newly arrived lady friend, but to listen to a mother cat teaching and admonishing her tiny kits is truly a joy. When one cat wishes to join another in a pre-empted place, such as a comfortable chair or sunny windowsill, both may comment in a monosyllable or two. If the first occupant wishes to reject the newcomer, he hisses and growls, and the newcomer promptly leaves. If the newcomer is permitted to join the first occupant, the newcomer will express his affection by washing the other's face and ears. (This is probably the nicest thing one cat can do for another.) Before long, they are washing each other. We have a crocheted cat bed on top of the television set and, quite often, when we are in the room, this bed is overflowing with four or five cats. Sometimes they are all washing one another at the same time.

Understanding Your Cat

Siamese cats are a constant source of wonder, challenge, and mystery. Of course, everybody knows that when a cat is annoyed he will switch his tail back and forth at a great rate. I am sure all owners of Siamese have seen their cats "pour" themselves out on the floor or in the sun. This means the cat is completely content and happy. If you pause and watch your cat and wonder what he is thinking or why he is doing what he is, you will soon

---

* I especially enjoyed reading *Translations From The Siamese*, by Warren Chetham-Strode.

Queen and prince of all they survey are DINAPOLI'S MISS AL-LA-BI and one of her kittens. Photo by Louise Van der Meid.

Head Study of a Blue Point Siamese. Photo by Louise Van der Meid.

DBL. GR. CH. DINAPOLI'S SERENADE IN BLUE. Photo by Louise Van der Meid.

Cats show their affection for each other by bathing one another; here shown in a demonstration of affection are DOCIA'S SCAMP-PI and his sister, both owned by Barbara Woods. Photo by Wm. Bond.

notice how often the phrase "When in doubt, wash" applies. When a cat hisses, he is merely expressing displeasure. It is not a danger signal but don't ignore it.

Different Colors Differ in Personality

Some of the noticeable personality differences among Siamese of different colors follow. Remember, however, that there are always exceptions.

Seal Points

I think Seal Points are the most extrovert in personality of all the Siamese, and I am sure they are the most independent. They are loving, but if you try to pick one up when he is busy doing something else, he will squirm until you put him down. These cats are real characters, often picking the man of the house as their special person. A Seal Point, with his dark points and light coat, is striking and he knows it. He often poses, and you can almost hear him say, "See how beautiful I am?"

Chocolate Points

My personal feeling is that a Chocolate Point is the most beautiful of all Siamese. That is, a good Chocolate Point, with his rich chocolate-brown points and handsome coat the color of cream, is every bit as striking as the Seal Point, and is of a gentler, sweeter nature. If they could, Chocolate Points would be perpetually in someone's arms.

Blue Points

A good Blue Point is an exquisite creature. I believe they are more loving than the Seal Points, generally. (Remember, there are exceptions in all colors.) If you're busy, don't be surprised to have your Blue Point jump up onto your shoulder (if he is a jumper and you haven't discouraged him from doing so as a kitten) and ride along with you so he can see what you are doing.

Lilac, or Frost, Points

These cats are fascinating in their own way, too. I believe there is not one in existence that isn't exceptionally loving. Each is a character, as are all Siamese. After people become aware that all Siamese are not Seal Points and see the other colors, they begin to appreciate the delicate coloring of these beautiful cats.

Frost Point male owned by Sol and Beatrice Gerlisky: GR. AND QUAD. CH. TA-LEE-HO'S FRO LIK OF RAMADA. Sire: Ta-Lee-Ho's Al-La-Bi; dam: Mi-Lana of Ta-Lee-Ho. Bred by Lavona Wright.

An unusual photo arrangement featuring three kittens owned by Clare Lapke.

Red Points, or Red Colorpoints

Breeders of this color tell me they are sensitive, mild, and gentle, and that they are the sweetest of all the cats they own. Breeders now have many Red Points that are breeding true, with the color and type continually improving. These cats could be nick-named "Patriotic," with their red points, white coat, and vivid blue eyes.

Albinos

Breeders of Albino Siamese tell me they are extremely affectionate, while being true Siamese in their monkey-like playfulness. They are as sturdy as any of the Siamese, and their litters are of normal size and number.

Red Point female owned by Mrs. N. Leoni, bred by Mrs. A. DeFilippo: GR. AND DBL. CH. SUNDUST SUDA FA YING. Sire: Sundust Daffodil; dam: Sundust Pink Pearl.

Chocolate Point male owned by Laverne Moss, bred by Werkle and Pfohl: QUAD. CH. SHEE-NWAH'S OKAI OF LOS GATOS. Sire: Red Wing's Cho-Abi of Elo-Yse; dam: Lao Ningpo's Tete-A-Tete. Photo by Rosa Gerok.

Curiosity and Climbing

The Siamese seem to be more curious than other breeds of cats. They love to climb up cupboard shelves, crawl into drawers and boxes, and pop into a closet the minute the door is opened. Opening cupboard doors draws them like a magnet. It is very easy to shut a cat in a cupboard or drawer without knowing it.

It is a common belief that Siamese cats climb drapes. I feel this is true, but of all the cats I have raised I have not had one that did this. If I see a kitten start to climb a drape, I give him a good swat with an emphatic "No!" and he doesn't do it again. Possibly the fact that there are other kittens and cats to play with and chase about has much to do with my success.

Watch Cats

When you know your cat, you will find he is every bit as good a watchdog as a dog, but he is much more quiet. Certain doorbells seem to ring only at their own discretion, which is not necessarily when someone on the outside is trying to ring them. Many times I have noticed all the cats sitting still, staring at the door expectantly, and I've opened it to find that someone had "rung" the out-of-order bell!

If you are sitting quietly in the evening reading, and your cat suddenly comes to attention, listening intently, then gets up and slinks over to a window, there is probably another cat or a dog outside, but it could be a prowler, especially if the cat is softly growling.

Cats often wake their owners when a room is filling with smoke or gas. Recently, I read of a Siamese cat killing a rattlesnake that got into his home while his owners were away.

Sneaky Siamese Cats?

Contrary to a belief all too common there is no such thing as a sneaky Siamese. If he appears to be sneaking about, he either is just playing or he is scared. If he wants something, he will try to take it right out of your hand. Actually, Siamese tend to be bold. If you leave a tempting little goody out on the table, and even though he knows he is not allowed up there, it is very difficult for a Siamese not to jump up and investigate it when you are not looking. Naturally, he will jump down if he hears someone approaching. I really don't think this is being "sneaky." (Children do the same thing. Are they "sneaky"?) Many of you have heard about, and many of us have seen, a Siamese snag a pork chop out of a pan while it is cooking. Often a Siamese will inveigle his way into your lap while you're eating, hoping you will share your food with him, and when you do not, he will try to snag it off your fork as you lift it to your mouth. (Is this "sneaky"?)

A Study in Ears

Have you ever seen several Siamese eating out of the same dish with their ears "folded" so they won't rub against those of the cats on either side of them? I am sure you have seen a cat listening to something, each ear independently cocked at a different angle, the direction of each continually changing as he tries to get a better focus on the sound.

Then there is the position of ears that makes a cat appear to be flying. When a cat peeks over something while playing, his ears will automatically go straight out sideways so they will not be seen sticking up above his head.

When a cat is angry, his ears are at yet another angle.

Siamese with "Seams" and "Stitching"

Have you ever really looked at a Siamese cat? He is put together with seams, so to speak. These are the ridges formed by the meeting of fur from two

Posing with his favorite toy, a stuffed lion, is a Blue Point male owned by Mrs. Fred Galvin: TR. GR. AND QUINT. CH. FAN-T-CEE'S KABAR KENNY. Sire: Kabar's Will-O-the-Wisp of Fan-T-Cee; dam: Fan-T-Cee's Tinker Bell of Kabar. Bred by Mrs. Fred Galvin and Ken Bartlett. Photo by Victor Baldwin.

different directions. Seams appear behind each ear, down the back of each hind leg, and there is a very noticeable one running down the underbelly until it parts to run to each hind leg. The top of this seam often is noticeable on the cat's chest. It looks like a "T." Where the "T" joins, there often is a tiny cowlick. When a cat is upset or angry the fur on his backbone stands up, and then it, too, looks like a seam.

While you're looking, notice the stitching effect on the muzzle. Out of each "stitch" grows a whisker—four rows of stitching, symmetrically arranged on each side of the nose leather.

An Active Cat

Siamese cats are usually quite active. They love to run and play and are delighted to play a game of hide-and-seek with you any time you take a minute to do so. It is most interesting to watch a Siamese jump up onto something: he will jump higher than necessary, literally selecting the exact spot where he

QUAD. GR. CH. JAKKI DALAI, owned by Virginia Daly, with some of his rosettes. Photo by "Muzzie."

Seal Point spay owned and bred by Margaret Hill Downs: R. S. QUAD. GR. CH. & PREMIER UPS 'N DOWNS JAH-DAH LING. Sire: Dbl. Ch. Ups 'N Downs Robin Wen Lu; dam: Ups 'N Downs Ka-Tiki.

wants to land while he is still in midair. If something that he couldn't see from the floor happens to be on that spot, he will somehow propel himself beyond or to the side of the unexpected object before landing. Watch, sometime, and see for yourself!

A Sad Note

Have you ever stopped to think what would become of your Siamese if you should have the misfortune to die suddenly? It would be very sad for a beloved pet suddenly to be without his home and your protection. Personally, I keep a list of my cats with our important papers on which I state just who is to have each cat, should something happen to us, together with appropriate addresses and telephone numbers. I revise this list from time to time as our cat family changes. As kittens arrive, I add them, the date of their birth, and who their parents are. Also, I note whether or not any of them is spoken for.

CHAPTER IV

HOW TO BUY A SIAMESE KITTEN

You have decided to have a Siamese kitten, and your decision is a good one. You haven't lived until you've been owned by a Siamese. They are almost more dog than cat. They love to ride in your car with you, and they are wonderful travelers. They can be broken to a leash. Their antics are straight from monkeydom, to the extent of having to be disciplined. Don't expect a Siamese to sit and sleep all day. As kittens, they are extremely active. They love nothing better than getting into mischief. This is a trait they carry with them throughout their lives.

Seal Point female owned and bred by Margaret Hill Downs: R.M. GR. CH. UPS 'N DOWNS SENA LING. Sire: Madali Thong Knao of Ups 'N Downs; dam: Ups 'N Downs Rhoda Ling. Photo by Rosen's Studio.

Wonderment, innocence, mischief, and intelligence are all wrapped up in these bundles of dynamic energy. Photo by Victor Baldwin.

Buy a Good Kitten

Breeding counts for a great deal in the enjoyment of your pet's beauty and personality. Most people are interested only in acquiring a pet, at first. This, of course, can evolve into a cattery and showing, as it did with us. But even if you want only one cat for your own enjoyment, buy a good one. As with everything else, you get what you pay for. Stop and think: you are going to live with this little one for quite a number of years. Select him carefully, and don't hesitate to pay a good price for him. Try dividing the price you pay by the ten or fifteen years you may expect to have him, and you will see it is negligible in return for the pure pleasure he will give you.

Be sure papers for him are available. I know, you just want a pet, but you will think so much of this pet before long that you will want to send for his papers. You will be proud to have him registered. Perhaps there will be a show in your city, and you will want to enter your Siamese. It is not necessary to have your cat registered to enter him in a show; however, if he wins a championship, he must be registered to claim it. As this book goes to press, one association, the Cat Fanciers Association, will not permit an unregistered cat to appear in any show it sponsors. (This is explained fully in Chapter V.)

How to Find a Kitten

Try the yellow pages of your telephone directory. If you find no catteries listed there, inquire at your pet store or an animal hospital. Ask someone who already has a Siamese where he found his. Obtain the names of several catteries, and visit each one. Persons who raise cats are happy to show you what they have available. Decide where you wish to buy. If one cattery doesn't have just what you want, it should be able to give you the names of several others.

Another suggestion on how to find a kitten is to attend a cat show, if possible. You then can see all the different colors of Siamese, which will help you to decide your color preference. The show catalog will list the name and address of the owner of every entry. *Cats Magazine*, which may be purchased at any cat show, is the only monthly publication devoted exclusively to cats. Many breeders advertise therein. You will find every issue entertaining and informative. There is an article each month called "Tips to the Novice." Show reports are in each issue, and there is a show calendar, listing all shows together with the date and place each will be held. Each of the several national cat associations usually has an ad. Anyone interested in cats will find this exclusive cat publication a must. This magazine is not sold on the newsstands. If you wish to subscribe to it, write to:

Cats Magazine,
4 Smithfield Street,
Pittsburgh 22, Pennsylvania.

Another monthly publication that will be of use to you is *All-Pets*, published by T.F.H. Publications, 245 Cornelison Ave., Jersey City, N.J. 07302.

Perhaps your petshop will have some Siamese kittens on hand, although most breeders do not put their kittens up for sale in a petshop. Instead, they usually leave their business cards with the petshop. Petshop proprietors will be happy to refer you to a breeder.

Usually, breeders prefer to meet the individuals who buy their kittens, and this is to the buyer's advantage. Feel free to call the breeder from whom you purchased your kitten for advice or information at any time. The breeder will be happy to help you. He is interested in the kitten making the transition to his new home and in having you as a satisfied customer. Breeders are genuinely interested in the welfare of their kittens. They love all cats, or they wouldn't be breeders.

You will be more likely to get a quality kitten from a breeder. They are continually trying special breedings in order to produce their own show stock for the ensuing season. Naturally, not every kitten is show type, and these are the ones you purchase from breeders as pets, or as breeding stock. The background and bloodlines are there and there is never a question as to availability of papers, which usually are sold for a $10.00 fee. You probably

Seal Point neuter owned and bred by Barbara Woods: R. M. NEUTER GR. CH. AND DBL. PREMIER DOCIA'S SCAM-PI. Sire: Coaley of Moon Glow; dam: Countess Ya Chai of Docia. Photo by Bill Bond.

will be interested in seeing the parents of your kitten, thereby getting a good idea of how your kitten will look when he is grown, and in seeing the rosettes and trophies your kitten's relatives have won.

Good-quality kittens are seldom advertised in newspapers. People who answer newspaper ads expect to find a kitten for $10.00, or even less, and breeders cannot afford to sell kittens at such prices. Think about it for a moment: anyone selling a kitten at such a price doesn't think much of the kitten or his own stock, for that matter. He is just interested in a fast buck and wants to sell the kittens as soon as possible. Needless to say, he's not likely to back his sale. That is, if the kitten should die in a day or two, the

Seal Point female owned and bred by Mrs. Fredric Hokin: GR. AND QUINT. CH. DARK GAUNTLETS IDOL. Sire: Ch. Tyoh Nusta of Dark Gauntlets; dam: Wah-Lee Nang Ty Dark Gauntlets. Photo by Hans Bomskow.

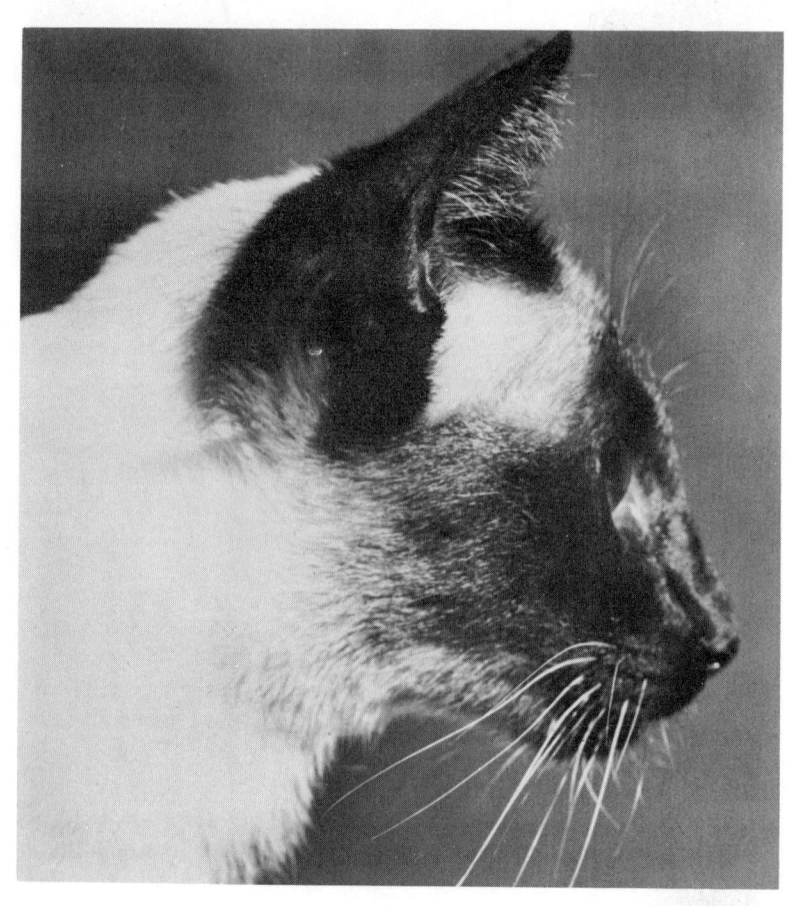

Seal Point male owned and bred by Miriam Williams: CH. SHA LIN'S PRINCE TAI TAO. Sire: Sha Lin's Pra Ping Thai; dam: Putta Song's P'R'N'S M'G'T R'S of Sha Lin.

unethical breeder's attitude would be, "I'm sure sorry, but the kitten was fine when you took him," and he would not replace the kit or refund your money.

An ethical breeder, on the other hand, will not, under any circumstances, let a kitten go until the kit is eight weeks old, at the very least. He would much rather sell a kitten after it has attained the age of three or four months. At that age, the kitten has had an opportunity to build up a little reserve to go on, he has had his feline enteritis and pneumonitis shots, and is much better prepared to leave his mother and adjust to a new home, new people, and different food.

What to Look for in a Kitten

A Siamese kitten should feel as compact as a paperweight. When you pick him up, he should feel solid and heavy, yet look lean and muscular, even at an early age. Never, never buy a kit with watery eyes or a runny nose. He may have only a temporary cold, but these symptoms may be danger signs. If you still want a specific kitten displaying these symptoms, ask the breeder to save it for you and call you when the kitten has recovered.

Discuss your particular requirements with the breeder. He knows the personalities of his kittens and is interested in making you a satisfied customer. He will make every effort to see that you get just the right one to fit your particular needs. It is quite a challenge to an ethical breeder to match a kitten and a buyer, personality-wise. It can be done; it often is.

After visiting several catteries, decide from which you want to buy. If the right kitten isn't quite ready, wait until it is. It is *not* wise to buy a kitten as young as possible. Many people feel a two-month-old kitten is too young to be taken away from his mother. He will be plunged into a strange environment, strange food, strange people, and quite possibly will be terrified. Perhaps he won't eat the new food offered right away. A too-young kitten hasn't had time to build a reserve of fat to fall back on, and if he goes off his food for a day or so he could be in trouble. You then would feel resentment toward the breeder and think he had sold you a sick kitten. Please remember you asked for the youngest kitten available. You assured the breeder you knew all about caring for him.

If you want to raise kittens, buy a female, breed her, and raise the kittens with her help. When buying, you will be very much wiser to look for a kitten that is close to four months of age. At this age, a kitten is well established, has a ravenous appetite, and won't go without more than one meal before eating almost anything placed before him. His personality, which is very important to you, has had time to begin to show. The breeder knows his kittens' tendencies by this time, and is in a position to know which one best will fit your needs. As mentioned before, by the time the kittens have reached this age, the breeders usually have had them inoculated against feline enteritis (cat fever) and perhaps pneumonitis. The cost of these shots is naturally included in the price you pay for the kitten, but you won't have to bother with several trips to a veterinarian; the kitten will have built up his resistance to these two killers and should present you with no problems.

What You Should Expect to Pay

Don't be afraid to buy quality and pay for it. You will be repaid many times in satisfaction. A good pet kitten should cost from $35.00 to $50.00. A good kitten for breeding should cost about $75.00. If you want a show-type kitten, expect to pay from $100.00 to $150.00. *"For a cat?"* I hear you say. How much would you expect to pay for a good pedigreed dog? "That's different," you answer. Well, how is it different? The breeder of the kitten has put just as much time, effort, and expense into producing the kitten as the breeder of the dog has in producing a good pup. I personally have known many who, after obtaining a good cat, gave up their dog and purchased another cat, better than the first. Ever-changing statistics indicate that the number of cat owners has probably surpassed the number of dog owners, and cat owners are steadily increasing. This fact is reflected in the increasing pet food ads directed at owners of cats.

At the prices mentioned above, a breeder is not making a great deal of profit. If you don't believe me, try it. Remember, I am talking about a good kitten, one who has many generations of good quality behind him. Beware

Blue Point male bred and owned by Mr. and Mrs. Howard Krebs: DBL. GR. AND TR. CH. KREBS INTREPID FOX. Sire: Krebs Don Juan; dam: Fan-T-Cee's Electra of Krebs. Photo by Victor Baldwin.

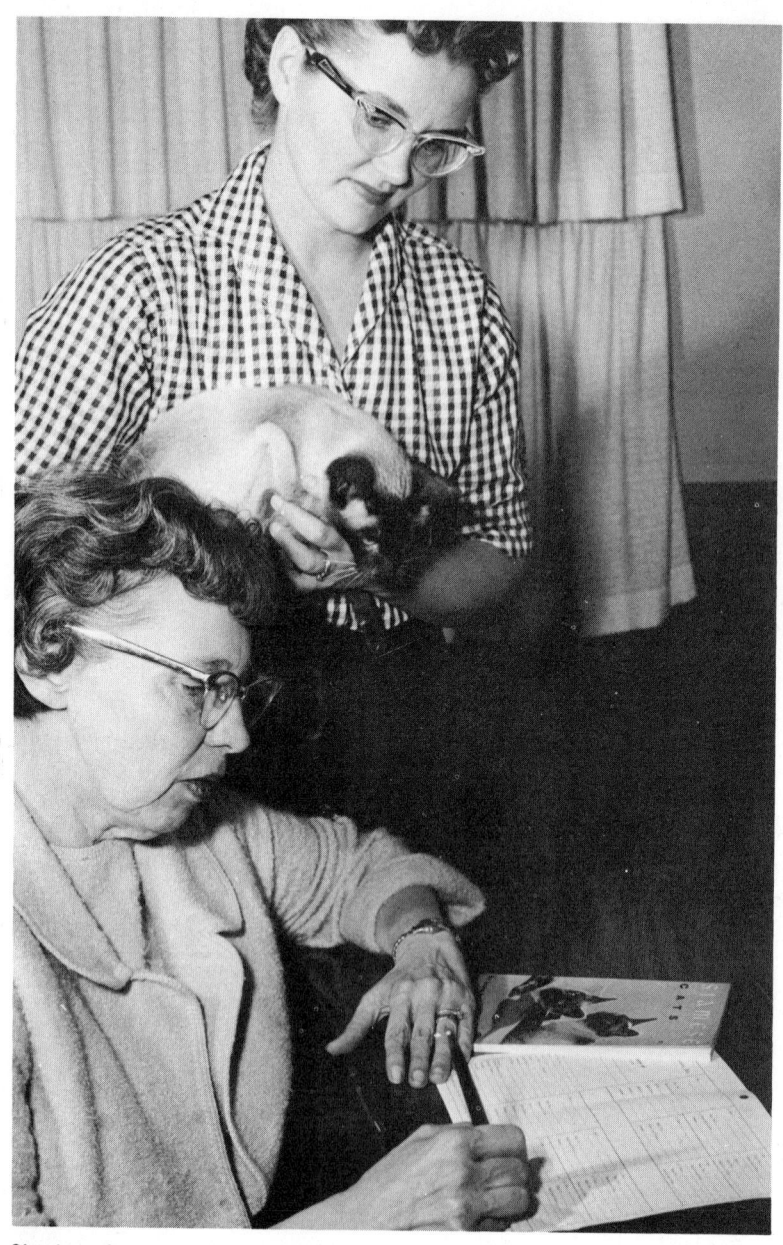

Signing the papers is more than a mere formality; it is an evidence of the breeder's good faith and enables the purchaser to have proof of the cat's ancestry. Photo by Louise Van der Meid.

of amateur breeders who have, possibly, found a Siamese, or at the most paid $10.00 for her, and located an equally mediocre male to breed her to in exchange for a kitten. These amateurs will tell you that papers are worthless. They are—to them. Papers should be available on any kitten you purchase. Many catteries litter-register all their kittens, thereby protecting themselves and paving the way for you, as a new owner, to register your own with the least amount of red tape. You never can tell when you might want to have papers. There should be several champion cats in the kitten's background, and even a Grand Champion or two. This background will all show up in the character, beauty, and health of your kitten.

Male or Female?

If you are buying for a small child, or if you plan to raise some kittens, you will be looking for a female. However, if you are certain you are not interested in raising kittens, and if you have no small children, then a male would be your best choice. I have found the males to be more intelligent, more loving, and more of a companion than the females. However, they are more a pet for an adult.

From this basketful of appealing kittens it would be hard to make a choice; a prospective purchaser would no doubt want more than one. Photo by L. D. Sample.

Why Alter Your Pet?

Regardless of which sex you choose, if you want a pet, only, your cat will be a much better pet if you have it altered at approximately eight months of age. Contrary to common belief, altering does not change a Siamese cat's personality or playfulness one iota.

You soon will find you just can't possibly stand the female's "calling" (screaming, actually), which usually goes on day and night for a week at a time when she becomes an adult. Before you know it, she is in season again, unless she has been bred or spayed.

If you do not plan to use your male cat for breeding, he will make a much nicer pet if he is altered, because when he grows up he will "spray." This you simply cannot have in your house, as the odor is highly objectionable. There is no use punishing him for this, for spraying is as natural to him as breathing. The operation required for altering a male is a minor one, and you both will be happier afterward.

I hear someone saying, "I don't believe in altering cats. Let them run and enjoy themselves." Did you forget you bought the kitten for a pet and a companion? If an unaltered male is running loose, he will be much more interested in roaming than in being the companion you thought you were buying. And have you thought of all the little unwanted mongrel kittens he will be siring? Quite possibly, these innocent little creatures will be dropped off to drown in a pond somewhere, or in the country to fend for themselves, or end up in some medical laboratory as experimental subjects. I don't want anything like that on my conscience. Do you?

Don't Let Your Siamese Run Loose

If you really love your cat and want him to enjoy health and a long life plan to keep him indoors. Your first reaction to that probably will be, "How cruel!" Again, let me remind you, you have bought a pet: do you want him lost, stolen, run over, poisoned, or mauled cruelly by another cat or a dog? And, needless to say, if your pet isn't permitted to run loose, he will not be tempted to catch birds.

Kittens purchased at a cattery have never been allowed to run loose. None of our cats ever have, and they all are healthy. I honestly believe they all are happy, too. If cats have never been allowed outdoors, they don't miss it. So often someone calls to say his beloved cat has just been run over, and asks if I have any kittens for sale. I have to bite my tongue to keep from saying, "If you had kept him in, you would still have him."

It is possible to train a cat to use the toilet, as is explained in detail in Chapter VI. This is quite handy, obviously, as it eliminates the necessity of a litter box. However, until your cat learns to use the toilet, he will need a litter

Siamese cats are innately clean animals, and even a kitten as young as the one shown here can be trained to use the litter box. Photo by Louise Van der meid.

box. The commercial deodorized litter obtainable at your pet store is the most satisfactory material to use in the litter box. All Siamese kittens are trained to use a litter box by the time they are old enough to be sold. Siamese cats are noted for their fastidious personal habits.

Two Kittens?

By all means, buy two kittens if you possibly can see your way clear to do so. Their antics will keep you constantly entertained. When you are away, they will have each other for company and will not be lonesome. However, if you can purchase only one kitten, don't hesitate to do so. Their adaptability to almost any environment and situation never ceases to amaze me. Don't feel you can't have a kitten because you work and the kit would be alone all day. I work all day, and I raise them. We actually find that when we are home on the weekends we are disturbing their routine and sleeping habits. If we go home unexpectedly during the day and go into the cattery, we find all the cats blissfully asleep, and we are greeted with soft protests for disturbing them. Cats are creatures of habit, and all cats like to sleep in the daytime. When the day's work is done and you are anxious to see how your Siamese is, you are greeted lavishly with affection and conversation.

If your landlord won't allow you to have a cat, move. You haven't lived until you have been owned by at least one Siamese cat.

Johnny Naples with his beloved pets, Phet and her granddaughter Pee Wee. Photo by Victor Baldwin.

A Suggestion

Buy a female kitten, raise her, and, when she's old enough, breed her and raise at least one litter of kittens. Out of this litter, keep one for company for the mother cat and yourself. This way you will have the priceless experience of helping to raise a litter of Siamese. Don't sell them too young. They are a "riot" when they are three and four months old. Friends will visit you to take pictures and to be entertained by the kits at play. If you purchased originally from a good breeder (who by this time is your friend), he may help you sell the kittens you can't keep.

What Color?

There are other colors of Siamese than Seal Point. All the different colors have been fully explained in detail in Chapters II and III. However, by visiting a cat show or several catteries before buying so you can see the different colors, you will be in a position to decide which you, personally, like best. You see the parents of the kittens, and should be able to tell what your kitten will look like when he has matured and has his full coloring. When small, a kitten will have a "smutty" coat. This is baby hair which will be replaced as the kitten grows. The smuttier the coat a kitten has, the better his color will be when he is an adult. However, certain bloodlines tend to darken, while others stay light; therefore, you will want to see the parents whenever possible. Their kittens will be like them when they are grown, and, probably, they will be even better specimens. When you buy from a breeder you are buying from someone who is constantly trying to improve his stock through selective breeding.

Teach Children to Care for Their Pets

If you are buying a kitten as a companion for a child, of course you will teach him how to care for the little fellow and how to be gentle with him. One thing quite often overlooked in training children in the care of cats is how to hold them properly. A cat should not be carried by the scruff of the neck. He should always be held by supporting his hind legs and rump as well as his chest. When a cat is being carried, his chest should be supported. He can be held against a person's body with the same arm that is supporting his chest.

CHAPTER V

CHOOSING HIS NAME AND REGISTERING YOUR KITTEN

You have acquired a little Siamese, and now you want to choose the right name for him.

Pet Names

Don't be in a hurry to settle on a name. As you get to know your kitten, a "pet" name will occur to you that is in tune with his personality, such as "Scrapper," "Imp," "Pee Wee," "Rocky," "Stinky," "Trouble," and on and on endlessly. You probably will always call him by the pet name. If you never register him, this first pet name will be enough; if you do, he will have two names, his pet name and his "fancy" name. Most of the time he will still be called by the former.

Of course, you may choose any name you wish. Perhaps you have a favorite name you want to use. Amazingly, a kitten usually grows into his name even if you very carefully pick out a fancy name or just choose something that sounds particularly good to you. It is sometimes uncanny how appropriate a name turns out to be. We named our first kitten "Phet," which in Siamese (Thai) means "uncut diamond." We had kept her because she was different from the rest. When we later learned that she was a Blue Point, we looked for a word in Thai that would, at the least, connote "blue." "Phet" was the closest we could find! She has truly been as precious and valuable to us as a diamond. She got us into breeding, clubs, showing, and the cat fancy. She is the foundation of our stock.

Use of Cattery Names

If you purchased your kitten from a reputable cattery and paid a good price, you probably have the pedigree or can obtain it later if you wish. If you enter either breeding or showing, you will have to register your cat. Or perhaps you just want to register because you are proud of your cat. At any rate, the name of the cattery from which you purchased the kitten should precede any given name you select. Possibly you are thinking of establishing

Frost Point female owned and bred by Margaret Hill Downs: DBL. GRAND & CH. UPS 'N DOWNS LIRIK. Sire: Flo-Mar's Yung Val of Bercrest; dam: Van Lyn's Tana Mera of Ups 'N Downs. Photo by Rosen's Studio.

a cattery yourself. Your own cattery name should follow the given name of any cat you have acquired. The registered owner of the kitten's dam (mother) is the breeder of the kitten. If you establish and register a cattery, then, of course, your own cattery name will precede any other name on all of the kittens you breed.

Length of Name Limited

Most associations permit a cat's name to contain only twenty-five (25) letters, including the addition of a cattery name. (The word *of* is not counted *when adding a cattery name*.) If a cat is already registered when you obtain it, you will want to add your cattery name, if you have one. Let me state this rule another way: if a cattery name precedes and succeeds a given name, the entire name may contain a total of only twenty-seven (27) letters (25 plus the "uncounted" two in the word "of") in most associations.

Example:
>Dulce Domum's El Coco of DiNapoli

Dulce Domum is the name of the cattery where the kitten was bred, El Coco is the given name, and DiNapoli is the name of the cattery that acquired

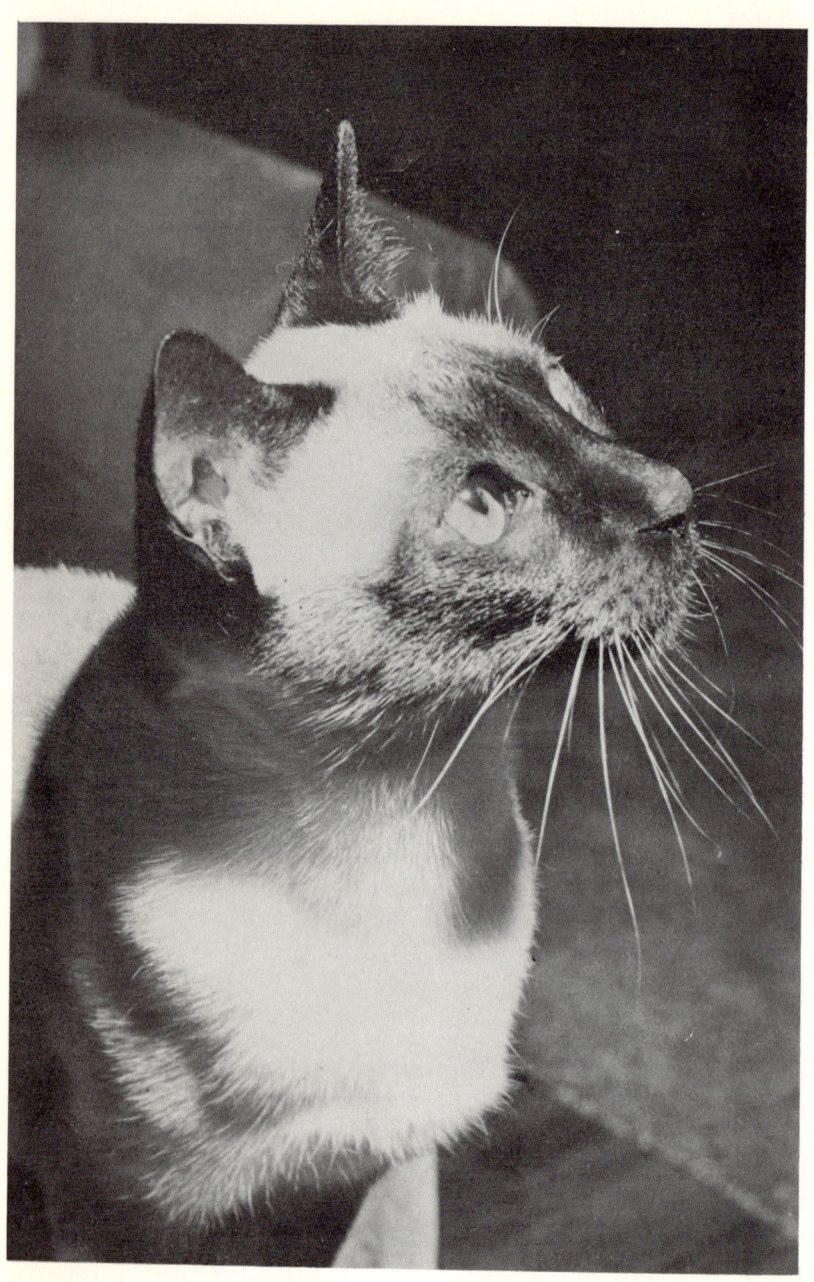

Seal Point female bred and owned by Esther E. Illingworth: DBL. CH. DEMBI'S MEI-LO-DI. Sire: Sha Lin's Pra Ping Thai; dam: Dembi's Suda Som Phong. Photo by Jeff Wiener.

Blue Point male owned by Grace Forrest and Jean and Bill Quiner: CH. BRIDLE TRAIL TIMOTHY OF BOGRAE. Sire: Bridle Trail Ping Mo; dam: Singa Godiva of Bridle Trail.

the kitten. However, this is only the end result. We had quite a time with this name. You will note the breeder's cattery name has ten (10) letters in it, and the "'s" adds another for a total of eleven (11) letters. The acquiring cattery name has eight (8) letters. Thus, nineteen (19) of the twenty-five (25) letters were used, leaving only six (6) for a given name! At DiNapoli Cattery, we have chosen "song themes" for the names of our male cats. This kitten was a Chocolate Point male. When you have a color other than Seal Point, you usually like to choose a name that implies the color. You can see that incorporating a song name that would imply chocolate in six letters was far from easy. We enlisted the help of a good friend who went to a music store and came up with a short list of chocolate-type names of songs consisting of six letters. Note that the full twenty-seven letters were utilized. Later on, we bought an album containing the music of *El Coco*, and it turned out to be the most delightfully happy, gay tune imaginable. Quite by chance, it fits the personality of the cat exactly.

The lesson to be learned from the foregoing is—if ever you must decide on a cattery name, make it as short as possible.

Thai (Siamese) Words With English Translations

Following is a list of Siamese words that could be used as names for cats, together with their English meanings:

Thai Word:	Translation:
Chaem Choi	Sweet Lady
Chai Chai	Siamese Dance
Chai-Lai	Beautiful
Chao-Fa	Crown Prince
Chome Chai	Beautiful Figure
Chuan Chit	Sweet and Attractive
Dara	Star
Dok Rak	Flower of Love
Fa Ying	Celestial Princess
Kla	Brave
Kumut	White Lotus
Naeng Noi	Sweet and Supple
Nai	Mister
Ngoen	Silver
Nim Nuan	Supple and Graceful
Nong Yao	Young Lady
On Choi	Suppleness
Phen Khae	Moonlit
Phet	Diamond (Uncut)
Phitsamai	Adorable
Phut Phat	Beautiful
Phut Son	Gardenia
Prija	Intelligence
Pundit	The Learned
Ratana Kanya	Lady of Quality
Rotchana	Lady of Beauty
Saeng Dao	Starlight
Saroj	Lotus
Sawat	Lovable
Sood Sawaat	Dearest
Sud	Tiger
Suda	Daughter
Thahan	Soldier
Thai	Free
Thong	Gold
Thong Khao	White Gold
Thong Kon	Gold Lump
Wila	Feline
Ya Chai	Sweetheart
Ying	Feminine
Yod Rak	Beloved

Registering Your Kitten

Many catteries litter-register their kittens by sending in the pedigree of the litter on the proper form, which must be signed by the owner of the kittens' dam, and the owner of their sire. They get back a slip for each kitten in the litter. This precludes sending in a pedigree on each kitten. When you purchase a litter-registered kitten, you will be given the kitten's slip, which contains the litter number, the kitten's birth date, and the names of its sire and dam. The breeder will sign the slip and list the kitten's sex and color. Also, you will be given the kitten's pedigree to keep for yourself. If you wish to register him, you will list your first, second, and third choices for his name, put your name and address on the slip, and send it along with the fee, to the address shown on the back. You will then receive a Registration Certificate giving the kitten's permanent registration number and name, which may never be changed, except for the addition of a cattery name. If you go on to show the kitten, be absolutely sure you enter him exactly as he is registered, and that your name as owner is the same as it appears on the kitten's registration certificate. Otherwise, he could lose any wins he makes.

We favor this method because we feel that the people buying a kitten should have the privilege of naming him; however, some catteries litter-register their kittens with names. In this case, you would be given the kitten's registration certificate with his pedigree, and you would have to send it in with a nominal fee to have yourself listed as the registered owner. Personally, I like the litter-registration program because it protects the breeder from misuse of pedigrees of valuable stock.

Catteries that do not use the litter-registration system give you the pedigree only; you will then have to make a copy to keep for yourself, sending in the original association form (we *hope* this is the form upon which it will be given to you). Some breeders will give you two copies of the pedigree, one to send in and one to keep for yourself. Most associations require the breeder's signature on the pedigree form before they will register a cat or kitten.

If you are buying a pedigree several years after you purchased the kitten, possibly your pedigree will be on a form the breeder may have on hand. You will then have to write to each association in which you want to register the cat and ask for the proper form to use, which they will send you promptly. (The addresses of all the national associations are listed in Chapter XIV.) Then you must copy the pedigree onto the appropriate form and send it in. However, if the cat is to carry the breeder's cattery name, the form will have to be sent to the breeder for his signature before it is submitted. Fees for registering kittens or cats vary among the associations. The back of each form lists the fee and the address for returning the form. The usual fee is $2.00.

Blue Point female owned by Mrs. Jolie Smith, bred by Mrs. Fred Galvin: DBL. GR. AND QUINT. CH. FAN-T-CEE'S SAPHIR. Sire: Kabar's Will-O'-the Wisp; dam: Ta-Lee-Ho's Minah. Photo by Victor Baldwin.

Which Association?

Registrations by the Cat Fanciers Association (CFA) are recognized by all associations because these registrations have been maintained in published stud book records since 1909. If a cat's name has been cleared by CFA, you will have no trouble getting the same name in any of the other associations. If you register with another association first, however, and then try to register the same name in CFA, you may find that the name already has been taken, or perhaps is someone's cattery name and may not be used, not even with your own cattery name preceding it. All you can do is choose another name to register the cat in CFA. You can readily see how complications might develop if you should forget which name the cat is registered in when filling out entry blanks for shows sponsored by other associations.

As I mentioned before, if a cat is not listed in a show catalog exactly the same as he is registered in the association sponsoring the show and the cat makes any wins, he may lose them. Further, in national competition, in which you may find yourself involved eventually, your cat might possibly be listed under both names and thereby lose part of his scores. If you get into national competition, you will need every point you can garner. You will learn all these fine points as you go along, so heed a word of advice and register your cattery and your cats and kittens in CFA first, and in any other associations you wish, afterwards.

When you buy a good cat or kitten, be sure his parents have been registered in CFA so that you will have no problem when you want to register him. Think of the heartbreak if you had an excellent cat and showed it, winning points toward a championship, but when you tried to register the cat in the association sponsoring the show (in order to claim the championship when it was completed), you found that that particular association does not recognize the registration of the cat's parents, registered elsewhere. This has happened. You may enter a cat in most shows, whether registered or not, but to obtain a championship he *must* be registered. Beginning with the 1962-63 show season, the Cat Fanciers Association (CFA)[*] requires that any cat being entered in championship or premiership (neuters and spays) competition must be registered in CFA before the entry will be accepted. Primarily, this is to eliminate the possibility of a cat's winning a championship and your then finding he is not eligible for registration.

Note: Beginning with the 1964-65 show season, **ACA** also requires registration before entry into competition.

CHAPTER VI

TRAINING YOUR KITTEN

Your kitten is an individual, and he goes through various stages, as do children. I like to refer to kittens that are between four and twelve months of age as "teenagers," for that is just how they act.* This is the period in which they should be trained to do the things you will expect them to do as adults. But be patient. They are full of spirit and mischief, and get into everything! This is when it is particularly nice to have a cage to confine them in when they get too rambunctious and you are too tired to enjoy such enthusiasm. If you discipline kittens during these formative months, you will find that you will be able to enjoy them much more during the years to come. I do not advocate abusing animals at any time, but you must be firm and consistent with whatever you are trying to teach them to do or not to do.

Be Gentle But Firm

I hope you did not buy your kitten expecting him to sit quietly all the time. This he will not do, unless he is sick. Be patient with him. He will settle down eventually, and fit into your habits amazingly well. He will even reflect your personality after a while.

Siamese cats are not naturally mean, but any cat can be made mean. Please, don't aggravate little kittens so they scratch and bite. It might be fun while they are little, but you are teaching them very bad habits. If you continually tease them, it will be only natural for them to strike back.

A Siamese cat can be a wonderful companion for a child. We bought a Siamese for our son when he was six years old. The cat, however, had ideas of her own and attached herself to the man of the house. We thought it would be educational for our son to let the cat have a litter of kittens. It was. We all became so intrigued with them that we evolved into a registered cattery.

Siamese are very tolerant of small children, as most cats are. They seem to understand that if children hurt them, they do not mean it. However, if the Siamese is a baby itself, it hasn't reached this age of wisdom as yet, and if it is

---

*The first year of a cat's life is hypothetically equivalent to twenty years of human life. Each year thereafter is equivalent to four years of human life. For example, a five-year-old cat is approximately equivalent to a thirty-six-year-old human.

A Siamese trained to a leash is much safer when going out for a walk with his mistress. Photo by Louise Van der Meid.

A champion Seal Point should have deep seal brown points of equal tone. Photo by Louise Van der Meid.

67

Seal Point Siamese. Photo by Louise Van der Meid.

The famous Frost Point male GR. CH. RED WING'S CHO-ABI OF ELOYSE showing his owner, Frank Magnan, how much he loves him. Photo by Louise Van der Meid.

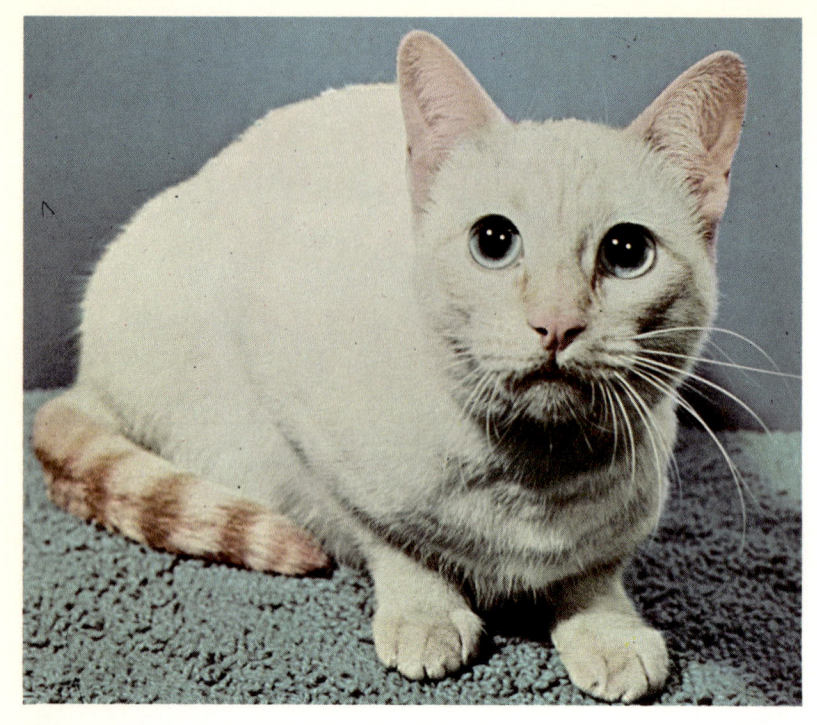

This Red Point Siamese has the typical coloring of the first Red Points; note bars on tail and lack of mask and color of ears, feet, and legs. Photo by Louise Van der Meid.

There should be a rosy flush to the points, especially the ears, of the Frost Point Siamese. Photo by Louise Van der Meid.

Chocolate Point female owned by Helen M. Kaufmann, bred by Vera Neilson: GR. AND DBL. CH. VELVET MITTS CO-CO CLOTILDE. Sire: Velvet Mitt's Pharoes; dam: Rasna's Akousa of Velvet Mitts.

squeezed, or its tail is pulled, it will turn and scratch with the speed of light. This is why some people feel a Siamese kitten is not a good pet for a small child. I would say it depends on the child. Some children love animals and are very gentle with them.

A word of warning here: if a cat ever turns on you, don't jerk your hand or arm away. This is what causes deep scratches and bites. The cat knows it is doing wrong, and will soon stop and run away. Disinfect your wounds and try to figure out why the cat did what it did. You probably will find an obvious reason. By all means, do not punish the cat. This will only make the situation worse. When I see a cat acting in a ferocious manner it never occurs to me that the cat is mean, rather that some human has made him the way he is. And it is sad. A cat should not be blamed for protecting himself. Would you punish children for fighting back when someone is picking on them? Actually, I feel cats have much the personality of humans, and, frankly, I prefer my cats to many humans I come in contact with.

A cat should be disciplined firmly and consistently. A little swat on the hindquarters with a folded newspaper, a loud clap, together with the word "No," or a well-directed squirt from a water pistol will soon get your point across. If you are trying to teach your kitten not to do something, stay with it.

By all means admonish him each time he does whatever it is. Don't let him get away with it some of the time and punish him for it the rest of the time. You will only confuse him. If you are consistent, he will learn.

Training to Stay Indoors

You have already read in Chapter IV of the sound reasons for keeping cats indoors. If you have decided to ignore such advice and let your cat run loose, skip this section.

If you have decided to keep your cat indoors, I would suggest that you never let him outside. As I have said, if a cat has never been out, he doesn't miss it. However, once he has been permitted to run loose, it is next to impossible to keep him from diving for the door each time it is opened. If he succeeds in getting out, he will take off with the speed of a missile; if he glances back and finds you chasing him, he will think it is a great game. It will be next to impossible to catch him until he is good and ready to be caught, which can be annoying if you are dressed to go out for the evening. Don't be angry with him. It probably is your own fault.

One book I recently read advised giving a swift kick once or twice to teach him not to dive for the door. I have never found it necessary to resort to anything so drastic. I can open the door with several kittens and cats sitting by watching, and they will continue to watch with great interest. On occasion, I have lifted one with my foot a short distance away from the door, saying, "No" in a positive tone. They soon come to look at the outside world as a big, noisy, terrifying place. This, too, has its advantages. If your cat should get out, he probably will be so scared that he will hide under a bush rather than take off at a full run and will hiss at anyone trying to pick him up, until you find and rescue him. Strange cats and dogs have great respect for the fighting ability of Siamese. They tend to leave them pretty much alone, especially if they are minding their own business and warning all comers to stay away.

Loose Cat!

If you do not go along with keeping your cat indoors, he will get along outside nicely, and love it, naturally. We let our first Siamese out when we left for work each morning. She was very happy sleeping somewhere when she wished, visiting all the neighbors, and fighting with all their cats. Although completely unaware of it at the time, we learned later that neither she nor we were what might be termed popular in that neighborhood. Some of our now-best friends we met after Smoky had been placed elsewhere. These friends, too, had Siamese, including one that ran loose. They lived several houses from us.

Seal Point female bred and owned by Eloise and Frank Magnan: TR. GR. AND QUINT. CH. ELO-YSE'S HI-VOLT-AGE. Sire: Encore Giselle of Elo-Yse; dam: Elo-Yse's Wing Sing.

They were away one day, having left a window open just far enough for their Ming to go in and out at will. Unbeknown to us, Smoky loved to pick on Ming. This particular day, Ming saw Smoky coming and dived in her window to what she had every reason to believe was safety. Needless to say, our aggressive Smoky dived in after her. Ming took refuge in a linen closet, high on a shelf of neatly stacked, clean linen. Many times since have I heard what a mess Smoky and Ming made of that linen. It's a good thing we weren't acquainted with Ming's owners at the time, as we probably would have ceased being friends then and there. Of course, if neither cat had been allowed to run, this couldn't have happened.

If your cat runs loose, I suggest you put on him a collar bearing your address and telephone number, and I'll tell you why:

A small velvet-footed cat on the loose attracts little attention. On the other hand, when a horse has lost his rider and is galloping free at horse shows and hunter trials, spectators quickly spot him and set up the cry "Loose horse! Loose horse!" alerting everyone to keep clear of the animal's unpredictable course. Instantly, a few experienced persons set out to corral the horse, lest he injure someone or himself, tripping over dangling reins or becoming frantic from a saddle suddenly slipped nearer his belly than his back.

But it's quite a different tale when a driver re-enters his parked car in which a curious little cat has crept unnoticed and curled up to enjoy the warm seclusion, and after a few blocks feels his backbone corkscrew and his scalp shrink at the weird long low wail from a spot behind him close to his corrugated spine. There had been no one to warn him with the cry "Loose cat!"

Now, if your cat wears an identifying collar bearing his address and telephone number (well, it's his phone, too!), and if the driver is a good soul (as most are) and able to relax after discovering a "wild" animal cowering on the back seat, he probably will either drop the cat off at your address or phone you. Rescued from the lost-and-found column: one beloved Siamese cat—yours.

Conversely, if the cat is terrified at this strange monster "stealing" him and hides himself to remain unnoticed, when the driver reaches his destination he will go off completely unaware of his stowaway. As soon as the cat feels it is safe to do so, he will jump out of the car. Whoever then finds him probably will call the telephone number on the collar and you, of course, will be happy to have located your pet and go to pick him up.

Believe me, many times have I seen a cat jump into a strange car. It happens often when there is no one to prevent puss's unscheduled trip away from home.

All cats, and especially Siamese, love to climb. If you put a collar on yours, be sure to put it on sufficiently loose for him to slip his head out if he gets caught on a nail or a branch. He would not be able to slip out of a harness,

A kitten's natural curiosity will prompt it to investigate many household furnishings and accessories, but cats and fish tanks usually don't mix well, as this young man is informing his kitten. Photo by Louise Van der Meid.

which is why I recommend a collar for the cat that runs loose. There are also expandable collars, available at your petshop, that will stretch and pull off should the cat catch it on something.

Training to a Leash

It is not uncommon to see someone walking his Siamese. For this purpose, of course, a harness is much better than a collar. If a collar were used for his walks, you would be pulling on the cat's neck, choking him, or dragging him by his head. I am sure you would never do such a thing, but I have seen it done. Be careful not to get hair or skin entangled in the buckle. Kittens should be at least several months old before you attempt to train them to walk with you.

First, let the cat get used to the harness, which may take several days. He will go through all sorts of gyrations trying to get that "thing" off, but soon something else will catch his interest. Before long he will forget all about it. After he is thoroughly used to the harness, it is time to venture outdoors with him. Snap a leash to the harness and carry the cat outdoors with you in the evening, after it is dark. As you know, cats are much more at ease outside when it is dark. Put him down on the sidewalk and let him investigate his surroundings. This is sufficient for the first night. Next time, keep him out a little longer. Let him become used to the grass, trees, and noises before you try to walk with him. This will probably take several evenings. When he is completely familiar with the situation, start walking with him. Use the words "Come," "Walk," and "No." If you meet a strange dog or cat, pick up your kitten and walk on by. Should the stranger be belligerent, your kitten would be at a great disadvantage with the harness and leash to hinder him. Besides, you don't want your pet in a fight anyway.

After he is used to walking with you at night, gradually get him used to doing so in the daylight. This will be greatly different to him, as it is the natural tendency of all cats to hide or slink along in a strange environment. There will be more noises, especially from traffic. If you want to take him across a street, I recommend that you carry him across and set him down to walk on the other side. If he balks at something or becomes frightened, pick him up and carry him until he is calm again.

I cannot go along with putting a cat on a leash and leaving him outside tied to a pole or clothes line. Strange cats, dogs, or children might decide to visit him, and he would be at a great disadvantage being tied up. Furthermore, this will get him used to being outside, and he will become discontented

Your cat will object to being placed in a harness at first but will soon lose his feeling of discomfort, and both you and your cat will benefit from its use. Photo by Louise Van der Meid.

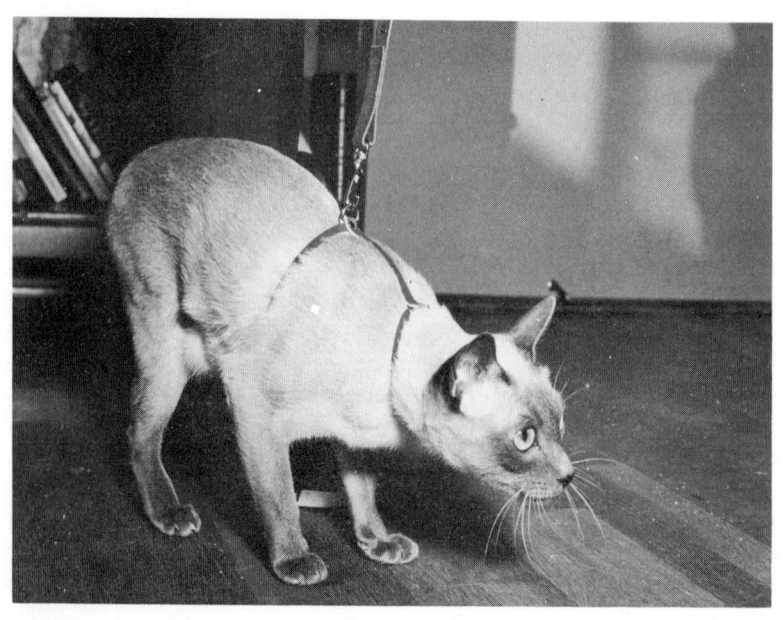

Seal Point male owned and bred by Virginia Daly: QUAD. GRAND CH. JAKKI DALAI. Sire: Newton's Tikena; dam: Ting Ke Ling Toi of Dalai. Photo by "Muzzie."

with being indoors. Taking him walking with you is different: you are with him and are at hand to protect him. He will come to look upon a stroll with you as a great privilege. It is not by any means the same as running loose.

Scratching and Exercise Posts

The first thing your new little one should be provided with is a scratching post. Many of the scratching posts on the market, however, are inadequately small; buy the tallest one you can find. It should be high enough so adult cats can really stretch when using it, to give their claws and muscles a good workout. The base of the scratching post should be heavy and broad to prevent tipping. Your little one will grow up, so you might as well start with a tall post. It is very easy to take off an old shredded piece of carpet and put on more whenever needed. Kittens will love to play and climb on the post.

A few years ago when we moved, we had 100% nylon carpeting put down in our new home. There were pieces left over, and when a scratching post needed redoing we used these extra pieces. It is the only kind of carpet the

The scratching post is an integral part of cat furniture. Scratching posts of all types are available at your local pet store; make sure that you purchase one large enough to accommodate your pet. Photo by Louise Van der Meid.

Chocolate Point male owned and bred by Mrs. Helen C. Koscak: GR. AND QUAD. CH. KOSCAK'S SUKI. Sire: Koscak's Luang; dam: Koscak's Starling. Photo by Paul Oxley.

cats haven't shredded in a matter of mere weeks. In fact, it has lasted on the posts for as long as a year at a time! When we made the move, we took along a big padded cornice board. As there was no place to use it in the new house, we tilted it against a wall, where it afforded our kittens and cats countless hours of unlimited fun. We left it for them to play on until it was almost bare. While it lasted, all of our cats, from the tiny babies to the adults, had a wonderful time with that simple contrivance.

Some cat lovers make very elaborate "poles" for their cats. These poles extend from the floor to the ceiling and have many shelves for the cats to lounge on, and even have a little house made for them at the top. Surely, cats living in homes so equipped are very happy cats.

At recent shows, we have seen some very intriguing furniture for cats. Two of their items are scratching devices. One is a pole made like the pole lamps that are so popular. It is covered with carpeting and has several shelves on which cats love to lie.

Another interesting item is named Cat Tapestry. A heavy piece of carpeting is suspended on any door by special hooks that hook over the top, and under the bottom of the door, in such a manner as not to harm the door. This could easily substitute for a scratching post.

You will find that cats consistently use their scratching posts. They stretch on them first thing in the morning, when they awaken. Whenever we let our cats out of their cages, they go directly to their scratching post and use it. All cats need to stretch their muscles to keep them in tone. This is primarily why you should provide your cat with an exercise post. He will use it with little or no training. Just show him where it is. Even though you have provided your cat with his scratching post, and he uses it regularly, you will find him using the carpet or a piece of furniture occasionally. He is very probably simply trying to get your attention, adverse though it may be, and it works remarkably well, doesn't it?

Blue Point female bred and owned by Mrs. Thomas Dugle: NIKE HAPPY TALK. Sire: DiNapoli's Duke of Fan-T-Cee; dam: Nike's Daphne. Photo by Lodder.

Red Point female owned and bred by Virginia Daly: GR. CH. DALAI RED MOUSE DEER. Sire: Sundust Amen Hotep; dam: Dalai Sukite. Photo by "Muzzie"

Teach Your Kitten to Retrieve

Many Siamese love to retrieve a crumpled piece of paper, an old sock rolled tight, or whatever. After they learn, they will wear you out demanding that you throw this toy for them. You can train your kit to do this in a matter of a half-hour or so, with a little patience and persistence. Keep throwing the toy for him. He will love chasing it, and when he plays with it rather than bringing it to you, go get it and throw it again. Keep repeating "Bring it." Before long, he will get the idea. Many people like to show off this trick to friends. They think it is great, if they don't have Siamese of their own that do it.

Toys

You can purchase any number of intriguing toys for your kitten from the pet stores. Ping-Pong balls are ideal. They are light to bat about, and cats get no end of enjoyment from them, as do all people who stop to watch. Small rubber balls that can be carried about in the mouth are also favorite playthings. Be careful that the ball is not too small, lest they swallow it, and

Your cat will spend hours on end playing with various toys. Safest of all toys are those sold in pet shops, manufactured expressly for use by cats. Photo by Louise Van der Meid.

the rubber should not be a spongy type that can break off and be swallowed. Rubber cannot be digested and may lodge in the intestines to cause much trouble. This same precaution applies to rubber bands. Do not permit your cat to eat them. For some reason, they seem to like to do so.

Catnip mice are a common favorite toy. However, we have found that Siamese are too rough for most catnip toys that are purchased. They have them torn apart and the catnip all over the rug in a matter of minutes. If you buy a catnip toy, find the sturdiest one possible.

Another favorite of kittens is the common foil we use so much today. It is easy to make a ball of a piece of foil. Kittens and cats will play with it for hours. However, a word of caution: pick up the ball of foil when the cats are finished with it, or at the end of the day. These foil balls soon become worn and pieces come off and the cats eat the pieces. This same warning applies to crumpled cellophane, such as cigarette package wrappers, and to tinsel from a Christmas tree, when it is that time of year. Any of these things can cause injury to the cat's stomach and intestines and, actually, death.

Pet stores carry many plastic toys for cats. These are fine, but it would be wise not to buy any made of a type of plastic that will crack or break should they get a part of the toy in their teeth and crush it. Plastic splinters in the digestive system are disastrous.

Cats love to play in paper bags. When I get home from grocery shopping, I put the big paper sacks on the floor and the cats have a wonderful time playing games in them. One day, I came home with several small boxes all the same size, and when they were emptied, I stacked them by the door so they could be taken out on the first trip outside. While eating dinner, we glanced around, and there was a cat sitting in each one, and the cat in the top one was having quite a bit of difficulty, as the entire stack was swaying back and forth! A similar and very simple toy for kittens is a large cardboard box with several holes and doors cut in it, placed upside down on the floor. Even grandmother cats will enter into the fun.

Training to a Litter Box

There really isn't any training necessary along this line. The kitten's mother has taught him to use the box. Just be sure the kitten knows where the box is. It is wise to keep it in the one place. Kittens, like children, wait until the last possible minute to stop playing and take care of necessities. If you had moved the box, the little one could hardly be blamed for having an accident. Siamese are fastidious; they appreciate a clean box at all times. If a box isn't clean, many cats will not use it. As soon as you change it, they will immediately use it!

Different materials may be used in the box. However, it would be wise to inquire from the breeder as to what kind of material the kitten is used to,

Situate the litter box in the area of your home most convenient for you, and keep it there so that the cats always know its location. Photo by Louise Van der Meid.

and use the same thing until you gradually change to what you prefer. For instance, a kitten accustomed to litter goes to a new home where the new owners, not having any litter, utilize shredded newspaper. The kitten has no idea what that is for and becomes very upset because he is unable to find his litter box. Many owners do use paper in the cat boxes. The main disadvantage to this, aside from odor, is if some papers were lying on the floor, what would stop a cat from using them? Still other people use wood shavings or sawdust. Most unsatisfactory is earth or sand. The commercial deodorized absorbent litter available at pet stores is by far the best material for the litter box. It is a bit expensive, but if you use it wisely it can be stretched to last quite some time. If you lift out the solid material with a tool for the purpose (available at petshops) or with a facial tissue, and flush it down the toilet and stir the litter around so that the damp parts can dry, I understand the same litter can be stretched for a week at a time, with only one cat using it. In this case, however, you would need quite a lot of litter in a deep pan. With multiple cats, we use only a little litter in a pan, and change it at least twice a day. Large catteries sometimes wash the litter with detergent and household bleach in a large barrel, rinse it thoroughly, and spread it out on a cement slab to dry in the sun. It is absolutely odorless when dry, and is used again and again. Beware of excessively dusty brands.

Training to Use the Toilet

Training a Siamese to use the toilet is entirely within the realm of possibility, and is most convenient, as it eliminates the necessity for a litter box. Some cats pick this up without any training. If you have one cat that uses this facility, others you acquire will soon follow suit. Your own imagination should indicate various methods of accomplishing this feat.

My husband made a little stool to fit into the litter boxes we use. This in itself worked out very nicely. The cats like these stools because they don't soil their feet; I like them because litter is not tracked all over the floor. Needless to say, we don't start kittens on these stools until they are four or five months old. Cats use their tails for balance and the little guys just aren't big enough to utilize the trainer stool. They get down into the pan and have a great time playing and digging. The older kittens and cats like a stool in their pan, and if the pan is placed in the bathroom, they simply make the transition by themselves when they are ready.

I am sure it would be no trick at all to teach cats to flush the toilet. All that would be necessary would be a sturdy string with a ball at the end attached to the handle. The cat could learn to pull down on the ball with sufficient force to flush the toilet. However, I'm afraid any cat would find this great sport and spend much of his time flushing the toilet. Rushing water seems to intrigue Siamese cats, and some are not afraid of water at all.

Intelligent and fastidious, cats can be trained to use the toilet, as shown here. Photo by Louise Van der Meid.

A further refinement of the litter box is to fit the litter box with a cover on which the cat can stand, thus allowing it to keep its feet out of the box. Photo by Louise Van der Meid.

Blue Point male owned by Mrs. Irving Cromarty, bred by Mrs. Remy Smith: TR. CH. JOLI'S PINNOCCHIO OF CROM-ARTY. Sire: Geppetto of Joli; dam: Fan-Tee-Cee's Flamboyant.

The Bathtub

We have had several kittens fall into the bathtub. They are so curious that they lean too far down to investigate and lose their footing. If this happens, grab the cat immediately and rub him as dry as possible with turkish towels, lest the bathroom be sprayed as he shakes himself trying to get the water off.

Many Siamese use the bathtub drain for their sanitary requirements when they have been inadvertently shut away from their litter box or when the box is soiled. Simply pick up the solid matter with a tissue and flush it down the toilet. Pour a little bleach down the tub drain, then scrub the tub. It is far better for a kitten or cat to do this than to use some remote corner, wouldn't you say? There are those who think it is terrible, of course. But is it, really?

Train to a Whistle

It is nice to train your cat to come when you whistle. This is useful, especially if he is allowed to run loose. A shrill whistle will carry quite a distance, and he will come running. Start by whistling when you call the cat to eat. He soon will associate your whistle with food and will drop whatever he is doing and run to you. Then try calling him by whistling, rewarding him with a tidbit of something he likes. Guests will think this a remarkable trick.

87

Train to Sit Up

Training to sit up is simple to teach and is effective when you want to show what your cat can do. He can sit up the same as a dog can, and he is able to remain so for long periods of time, using his tail to balance. This trick is taught at feeding time. Hold the cat's plate of food just above his head and say "Sit." Repeat this until he does sit. Have him sit each time you feed him. He will soon become expert and do it with no effort at all, being happy to sit for you on command whenever you hold up a tidbit for him, completely ignoring an audience.

GR. AND TR. CH. PUR SANG SI'S FU FU FOUJITA finds something very interesting and sits up to reach it. She is owned by Clare Lapke.

Cats are good travelers and enjoy going on car excursions; sometimes, as when traveling to a show or in the case of a cat who is not used to car travel, it is best to keep the cat confined in the carrier during the trip, letting him out for occasional exercise. Photo by Louise Van der Meid.

Car and Boat Training

It is most enjoyable to be able to take your cat with you on short or long trips. One of the particularly nice things about Siamese cats is that they are wonderful travelers. Most of them enjoy riding in a car, especially if they started while young. If the outing is to be only an hour or so, it probably won't be necessary to take a litter box along. If it is to be an all day trip, and the cat may be required to remain in the car while you visit someone who doesn't particularly care for cats, it would be wise to put a litter box in the car. The floor of the back seat is usually a good place. In a station wagon, you should be careful to place the litter box so it won't be sliding the length of the car each time you apply the brakes. We just leave a litter box in our car, and when we are going somewhere we don't have to stop and fix one to take along. If you leave your cat in the car, I'm sure I don't have to remind you to lock the car, first making sure to open the windows an inch or two from the top for ventilation. Don't open the windows far enough for either the cat to get out or anyone to get in to visit him. It is preferable to have a carrier along, as he will be happy to curl up and sleep in it while you are gone. Be sure to find a shady place to park if you are going to leave him in the car. If it is a blistering hot day, you really should leave the cat at home.

One of our cats has been trained to go on our boat. At first he was horrified, and climbed into a small secluded space and would not come out until we dug him out to take him home. Now he is an old salt, purring all the time he is aboard. Even while at the dock he makes no effort to get off the boat. This was accomplished by taking him along a couple of times when we went down to the boat just to get something, and again when we went down to start up the motor and run it awhile. By then he was on familiar ground, and when we took him out next time, he climbed up high where he could see what was going on, taking in everything. This was a night trip, and he loved it. Needless to say, we will always take him. He is proud and happy to be with us.

Vacationing With Your Cat

You will become so attached to your Siamese that you will want to take him vacationing with you. We wouldn't think of going on vacation without one or several of ours. We have found Siamese cats to be great travelers. It is fun having them along. You will be surprised to notice how many people travel with their cats. We take a small suitcase just for our cats' supplies. It contains quite a few cans of food, a sturdy dish for water, paper dishes for food, can opener, spoon, rubber brush, flea comb, harness, leash, a cat sweater, litter, disposable litter boxes, and a clean towel or two for the bottom of the carrier. That about does it. We always take a carrier for each cat, their "homes away from home." They sleep in them in the car, by their own choice. You know a cat is safe if he is shut in his carrier when you are loading and unloading the car.

After you are on the road, let your cat out of the carrier. He will roam around the car awhile, then settle down in your lap or on the seat beside you and spend most of the trip there. You will be amazed before long to note that he knows he should stay in the car. At the motel or hotel, inquire as to whether or not the cat will be permitted. Some do not permit pets; most do. It is better that the management knows you have your cat along than to be sneaking around trying to keep his presence a secret, when it would be your bad luck for him to set up a loud fuss about something in the middle of the night.

After you have all your luggage in the motel and are ready to stay put for the night, inspect the rooms to see there is nothing the cat can get into that could harm him. (Recently, I had occasion to take a quick business trip, and, of course, took one of our cats along. Luckily, I looked the motel room over before letting the cat out of her carrier. In the bathroom under the sink, was a hole in the wall just large enough for her to have crawled through!) Of course you will have brought the litter box in with you and put down the water dish and food. The cat will roam around for a few minutes, romp and play a little while, eat, and then settle down to sleep for the night.

You may take your cat on the train with you, if you purchase a compart-

Frost Point male (left) owned and bred by Lt. Col. and Mrs. Louis Pearson: VENTURA T'AN TS'IEN. Sire: Ventura Caballero; dam: Madalie Fleurette of Ventura. Chocolate Point female (right) owned by Lt. Col. and Mrs. Louis Pearson, bred by Madeline Christy: QUAD. CH. MADALI FLEURETTE OF VENTURA. Sire: KoKoKhan of Madali; dam: Kalyan Valerie of New Moon. Photo by Herb Topy.

ment; otherwise, he must ride in the baggage car, in his carrier. Usually you may go in the baggage car to see that he is all right. If you are traveling by plane, you can check the cat, in his own carrier, at an excess baggage rate on your ticket. He rides on the same plane with you, thereby arriving when you do. He will be in a special compartment which is pressurized and heated for animals. It is always wise to make reservations for the cat at the same time you make your own. It is my understanding that airlines book only a limited number of animals on each plane. The policy of one airline contacted recently regarding letting an owner keep his cat with him in the passenger area was as follows: If reservation is made well in advance to insure that only one animal would be in the passenger area at any given time, it would be permissible for the owner to have the cat, confined in carrier, in the cabin with him.

Carriers

There is little "training" involved in putting a cat in a carrier. Some cats object strongly, but there are times when a carrier is the only way to transport a cat. When being taken to a veterinarian, or anywhere, when he is not used to riding in a car, it is practically a necessity to have a carrier in which to confine a cat. If you have cats other than your own in your car, as when going to a show, each must be confined to his own carrier, or you may never make it to the show. A great fight could break out and the driver would be hard put to keep his eyes on the road. A cat should never be permitted to be under the driver's feet or entwined in the steering wheel.

When shipping a cat, a carrier is a necessity. If you have your own, you will not have to rent one from the airline, plus paying the charges for shipping. When taking a cat to be bred, it is much easier to have her in a carrier. When she arrives at the strange cattery, she will be in a panic upon seeing so many strange cats and being assailed by unfamiliar sounds and smells. If she is safe in her own carrier, there is no danger of you or anyone being scratched trying to handle or catch her.

There are many types of carriers obtainable at pet stores. The most common is the type constructed of strong wire mesh. These are good utility carriers. There are also plastic carriers, and while at first glance you may think these

The wire mesh carrier provides maximum ventilation. Photo by Louise Van der Meid.

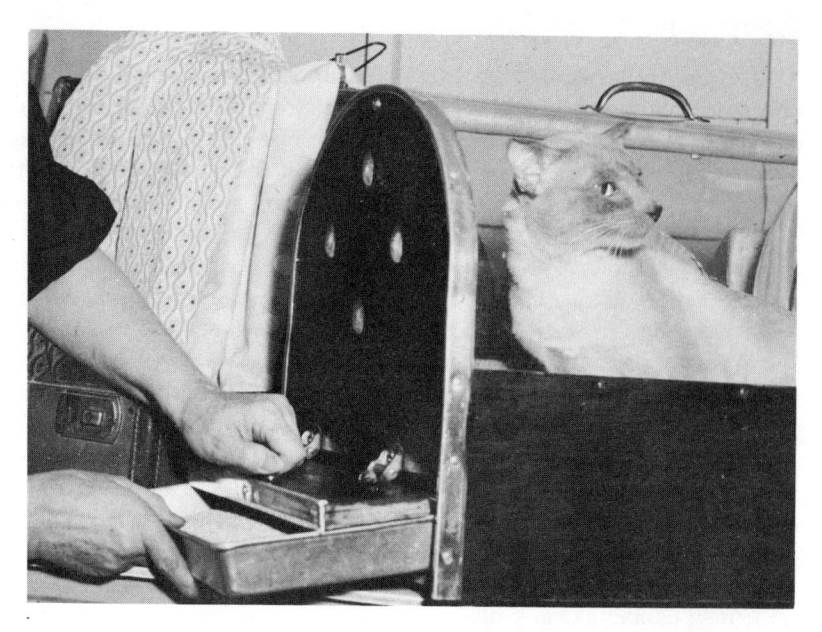

This carrier is equipped with a litter tray, making sanitary conditions easy to maintain. Photo by Louise Van der Meid.

would be the best, it is debatable, for plastic is hot. I have had cats get carsick in plastic carriers, whereas they never had in any other type of carrier. There are carriers that resemble crates, good because they stack conveniently. You will find in traveling with your cat that this type is more versatile than those that are rounded.

A good sturdy crate-type carrier is ideal for shipping cats. My favorite kind is made of pressed cardboard. It is very light in weight, has vent holes on both ends, and yet is surprisingly strong. Cats like to be hidden when they are in strange surroundings, and it is dark inside this type of carrier. I have used this kind for one of our show cats for several years, and it has had hard use, having been shipped many times by air and by train. If you use the open-mesh type to ship your cat in, cover it with a piece of blanket or cloth, because short-haired cats get cold easily on windy runways and train platforms, and many baggage cars are not heated.

When you are buying a carrier, choose one that is medium in size. If you get one only large enough for a kitten, it won't be long before you will need to buy a larger one. If you use a huge carrier, you soon will find it is too heavy and takes up too much room, and it would cost a great deal to pay for all that extra shipping weight.

Shipping Your Cat

There is no particular training required in shipping, but we have been discussing carriers and traveling, so it seems appropriate to mention shipping of cats, also. Most people prefer to ship animals by air, since they are en route much less time than by any other means. Make a reservation with a specific airline for the cat you are shipping, and check with them as to the type of carrier they will accept. Also, check to see if the cat will require a health certificate before being accepted for shipment to its destination. Some states require health certificates, others do not. Your veterinarian, also, can tell you which states require health certificates. If one is needed, he will examine the cat and fill out the forms required, for a nominal fee.

I suggest you feed the cat lightly two or three hours before flight time. Give him plenty of time to utilize his litter box before confining him to carrier. Putting a small litter box in the carrier is debatable. I used to do so, and never found the litter used. Possibly a better idea is to fill the bottom of the carrier with shredded paper, if the trip is one of many hours. I always put in several thicknesses of soft toweling so the cat can curl up and sleep comfortably. If the cat being shipped is particularly high strung or nervous, it is sometimes desirable to give him a tranquilizer before checking him in at the airport.

It is more economical to ship via air express than by air freight. Air express charges are for the actual poundage of the carrier and the cat, while air freight charges are for a minimum of fifty pounds, and fifty percent additional for animals. An office of the Air Express division of Railway Express Agency (REA) is located at most large airports. It is a good idea to check with them as to the exact airline on which the cat will be shipped and his time of arrival at his destination. Either wire or call whoever is to meet the cat and give them the time of arrival, airline, and the number on the express receipt. If something happens that the cat doesn't arrive as scheduled, he can be traced from this number. It is always a relief if the person receiving the cat wires or calls the shipper to let him know that the cat arrived safely. Another tip: ship the cat collect. Recently a well-known shipping agency charged me when I picked up a cat I knew had been shipped prepaid. Eventually, a refund was obtained, but it took needless time and inconvenience. Somehow, I feel that if a cat is shipped collect it may receive better care en route. Likewise, I insure a cat for several hundred dollars, hoping he may receive more attention on the way. The cost for this is nominal, approximately eighteen cents per hundred dollars.

Cats usually receive good care, but I always feel I am being cruel when I lock a cat in a cage and send him off, helpless, in the care of strangers. If the trip involves being gone overnight, attach a little sack containing a can of the food you want him to have, a little plastic jar of water, and two disposable

Chocolate Point kitten owned and bred by Mrs. Don Hoggendon: DBL. CH. ALMAR'S CUPCAKE. Sire: Sha Lin's Pra Ping Thai; dam: Sha Lin's M'Selle of Almar. Photo by Miriam Williams.

dishes, one for the food and one for his water. Different water often upsets a cat, as it does you when you are traveling.

Introduction to a New Home

All too often, the kitten is subjected, upon its arrival at its new home, to fondling and carrying by each member of the family, even being brought to the neighbors for similar treatment. The poor kitten is scared, confused, and quickly becomes very tired. He finds himself in a strange place, all the humans around him are strange, and his mother, his brothers, his sisters are nowhere to be found. Someone offers him food he never saw or smelled before, and he doesn't want it, anyway. Well, don't be surprised if he jumps away, hissing, and races off to the darkest corner he can find, refusing to come out.

Blue Point male owned and bred by Mrs. Joli Smith: DBL. GR. & QUAD. CH. JOLI'S STARFIRE. Sire: Joli's Geppetto; dam: Fan-T-Cee's Flamboyant. Photo by Victor Baldwin.

Chocolate Point male owned and bred by Mrs. Helen C. Koscak: GR. AND QUAD. CH. KOSCAK'S CHOCO-CHING-LING. Sire: Koscak's Suki; dam: Koscak's Star-Ling. Photo by Gordon Laughner.

First of all, when you are introducing a kitten to a new home, confine him to one room, making sure a litter pan and food and water are there. Leave him alone until he becomes somewhat acquainted with his new surroundings. After a day or so, when he has become accustomed to the new smells and noises around him, let one member of the family make friends with him, feed him, hold and pet him. After that, leave the door to his room open, and allow him to venture out into the rest of the house and to the people in it, whenever he is ready. He soon will be right at home. If the kitten refuses to eat or becomes listless, call the breeder from whom you purchased him and ask what you may be doing wrong. He probably will be able to tell you, and the kitten will thrive. Breeders are deeply interested in their kittens' making successful transitions to new homes.

If there is another pet in the house, let it and the new arrival get acquainted while you are with them. The other pet may claim squatter's rights and resent your bringing in what he feels is a replacement for him. However, after a few days of curiosity, their desire to play will assert itself and they will soon become fast friends. Don't be alarmed at a great deal of hissing and spitting. This is only natural, and usually mere bluff. An older cat will adopt a kitten and take care of it for you, and although it may surprise you, Siamese cats get along with dogs remarkably well.

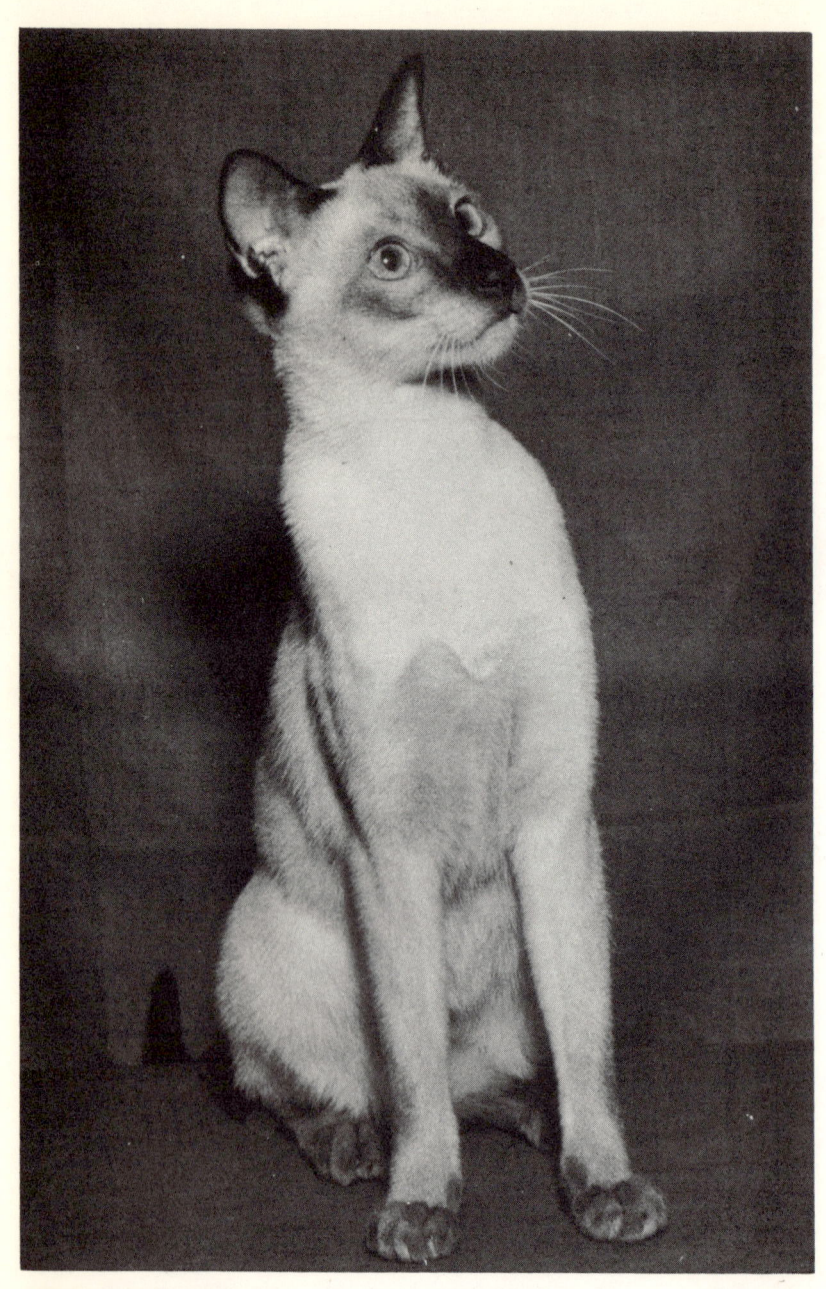

Chocolate Point female owned by Miss Cherise Thrift, bred by Sue McNally: R. M. GR. CH. GIDGETTE OF CYRECCIA. Sire: Green Lane Van of Velvet Shadow; dam: Cyreccia's Terrimina.

Frost Point male owned by Madeleine Christy, bred by Mrs. A. Hargraves: R.M. DBL. GR. & QUINT. CH. LAURENTIDE THIO (IMP) OF MADALI. Sire: Laurentide Mercury; dam: Laurentide Ephree Amethyst. Photo by "Muzzie."

A Safe Home?

Our homes, which we believe to be perfectly safe for our pets, harbor a variety of potential hazards:

House Plants

House plants such as philodendron, rhododendron, bouquets with mountain laurel, African violets, and other plants with woody stems, are proving poisonous to cats that nibble on them. Philodendron has now been placed in the poison ivy class, as there have been a number of philodendron poisonings, with a high fatality rate. Don't take any chances.

Cats love to nibble on the flowers and plants and invariably tip them over, often breaking a vase, always spilling the water or dirt, as the case may be. They love to dig in the dirt, whereas I am not fond of cleaning it up; therefore, I have given up having cut flowers and plants in the house.

Oleander Shrubs or Trees

The long thin leaf of the oleander is poison to both cats and humans. Either cats or children could be playing with these leaves and decide to see how they taste.

Christmas Trees

Cats love to pull the tinsel off Christmas trees and chew on it, invariably swallowing some. A Christmas tree is very interesting to feline members of the family. If it is a real tree, be sure to have it on an extra sturdy base, because when you're not looking your cats may take the opportunity to see what's on the upper branches, and chances are the tree will be toppled over before long. The easiest way to avoid trouble is to confine the cats elsewhere in the house, except when you are in the room with them and the tree. We soon learned to put the unbreakable ornaments on the bottom branches, and no tinsel within easy reach of forepaws. Eventually, we purchased an all-steel tree which is reusable each year, and upon which lights can be put directly, whereas they can't be used on an aluminium tree. Our main reason for purchasing the artificial tree was not exclusively for the benefit of the cats: we love our forests, which are fast disappearing; if everyone had a reusable tree, the annual slaughter of young trees would be halted.

CH. KANNIKA OF MADALI owned by Mrs. Madeleine Christy, bred by Mrs. Eleanor Hamling. Sire: Rosemar Yu Tang of Madali; dam: Kalyan MoKa Mo Lin. Photo by "Muzzie."

Frost Point male owned and bred by Mrs. Madeleine Christy: QUAD. CH. MADALI TAI SHAN. Sire: Laurentide Thio (IMP) of Madali; dam: Sable Silk Tanja of Madali. Photo by John White.

Shoulder-Riding
   While carrying a cat around on your shoulders is fun for both the owner and the cat, it does have a dangerous aspect. A cat used to jumping on his master's shoulder will do so whenever he feels so inclined, and if the person is not prepared for the cat to jump, he could be scratched badly. Suppose while you were carrying a kettle of scalding water, a cat unexpectedly jumped onto your shoulder, throwing you off balance: one scalded human and one scalded cat.

Refrigerator Doors
   All cats love to be underfoot while you are preparing food. When a refrigerator door is opened, the cat will be right there to see what he can find. If you were to swing the door shut without looking, it could catch his head or his tail, and cause serious injury.

Seal Point male owned and bred by Miriam Williams: DBL. GR. AND QUINT. CH. SHA LIN'S PRA PING THAI. Sire: Millbrook Ping Pong; dam: Sha Lin's Princess Da-R-Ling.

Electric Cords and Plugs

Teach your kitten not to chew electric cords. At about four or five months of age, a kitten loses his baby teeth and cuts his permanent teeth. It is only natural for him to chew on almost anything while he is teething. Electric cords seem to him to be especially nice for cutting teeth. The danger is obvious. A kitten could easily get a severe shock or burn if the cord has current running through it. If an inquisitive paw is poked into an outlet, a bad shock could result.

Washers and Dryers

Several friends have related how their beloved cat got into the clothes loaded in a washer, and when the machine was turned on met a horrible

Head study of a Seal Point Siamese. Photo by Louise Van der Meid.

Head study of a Frost (Lilac) Point Siamese. Photo by Louise Van der Meid.

Mother Siamese display a remarkable control over their offspring and seem to have an immediate knowledge of any trouble their kittens are getting into. This kitten was caught in the act, as its expression shows. Photo by Louise Van der Meid.

Dogs and cats, contrary to popular belief, are not natural enemies; they will get along with one another if given a chance. Photo by Louise Van der Meid.

Seal Point female owned and bred by Mrs. James D. Ramos: ISMENE'S GAL-X-CEE. Sire: Fan-T-Cee Tee Cee; dam: Krebs' Patricia of Fan-T-Cee.

death. Nothing can be done to bring them back to life; care should be exercised in use of a washing machine, and all side-loading machines, in particular, should be carefully inspected before closing the door. Cats should be locked out of the laundry area on wash day. Cats have died in dryers, too—and in instances where children have put them in, utterly inexcusably.

Insecticides

As will be discussed in Chapter IX, under the section on poisons, be very careful of the sprays you use in a closed room, and be especially careful about letting a cat out after you have sprayed your lawn with insecticide. It is poison, and cats love to eat grass.

Sleeping Habits

Many of us like to let our cats sleep with us, and why not? I think this is where they should sleep. There is no cleaner animal, especially a cat that is kept indoors. However, some people do not approve of this. So show the kitten where his bed is and be firm in not letting him join you when you have gone to bed. He will try. Be consistent. If you don't want him to sleep with you, don't let him do so occasionally and then expect him to sleep elsewhere unprotestingly the rest of the time. Cats love to have a cave-like atmosphere

Seal Point male owned and bred by Helen Arthur: THANI TAO CHI TU. Sire: Kalyan Cha Mo; dam: Wolfgang Liebsti II of Thani. Photo by John H. White.

Frost Point female owned and bred by Mrs. Madeleine Christy: CH. MADALI MYOWNE LILACIA. Sire: Carousel Opalesce; dam: Laurentide Solitaire (Imp.) of Madali. Photo by "Muzzie."

in which to sleep. This is true for cats in the jungle as well as in your home. If you have many cats and can't buy beds for all of them, a cardboard box from the grocery store will do. In the winter when it is cold I cut a door in a box and then place it upside down so the cat will be warmer, putting in old towels or pieces of blankets for them to cuddle up in. It is easy to wash these cloths. Cats love company. If you don't permit yours to share your bed, then the ideal situation would be for him to have another cat to sleep with. If you have just acquired a little kitten and there is no other feline for him to sleep with, put a ticking clock under the blanket in his bed. He will feel he is not alone, and so will sleep.

Cats sleep the greater part of the day and it is nice for them to have their own bed. We recently won a crocheted cat bed with a rim of about an inch and a half. It is amazing how much it has been used. All the cats love it. They like to sleep on top of the television set when it is on because it is warm there. We put the crocheted bed on the television for them, and often there are a few cats in it. When I'm working in the kitchen, I put this bed on top of the refrigerator for them, and they love to sleep in it up there, too.

Wool-Eating Cats

Although I never have had a wool-eating cat, it must be quite a problem. Perhaps this habit stems from a lack of vitamins and minerals in the diet, or from a kitten's having been taken from its mother too young. At any rate, other breeders tell me that it can be controlled by the addition to the diet of pure lanolin, obtainable at drug stores. While I don't know how much "science" has gone into this cure, it seems logical. Lanolin is derived from sheep's wool. Worming has been known to cure the habit. Giving a cat dry food to chew sometimes seems to satisfy the craving. It seems to me that all three would be less expensive than one cashmere sweater.

Cats and Asthma

If you have asthma or hay fever but still love cats and really want one, it is possible for you to do so. I am speaking from experience as I have a very

Seal Point female owned by Peita Boutelier, bred by Marge Naples. ROYAL MERIT CHAMPION DiNAPOLI'S PENNEY SERENADE OF BOUTE. Sire: DiNapoli's Serenade in Blue; dam: DiNapoli's Ratana Kanya. Photo by W. J. Thomas.

Chocolate Point male owned by Miss Cherise Thrift, bred by Mrs. Rex Naugle: R.M. DBL. GR. CH. GREEN LANE VAN OF VELVET SHADOW: Sire: Green Lane Vance; dam: Doneraile Brun of Malvana.

serious asthma problem, yet I raise Siamese cats. I have an understanding physician who realizes how much my cats mean to me, and he has worked with me so I can have them. I suggest you get a Siamese cat, because their fur is so short and close-lying. Your family could help a great deal. One of them could brush your cat for you outdoors, every day. This would cut down the amount of hair flying about the house. It would be wise not to permit your cat to sleep with you, in this case; better still, not to permit him to go into your bedroom at all. With an asthma problem, you probably are treating it anyway. Don't let your doctor or any of your friends tell you your cat, alone, causes your asthma. The cat may aggravate the condition that already exists, but so do many other things. A good doctor usually can raise your tolerance level for all of these things to a point where you can enjoy life and your cats.

Dress Up Your Cat

Many pet stores stock the ever-increasing number of items of clothing for cats. There are sweaters to keep them warm if it is chilly or damp outside when you want to walk them or take them riding with you. Remember that Siamese originated in the tropics and any whose coat is particularly short chills easily.

Cat clothes come in a multitude of styles and colors; cat sweaters are particularly useful, as they serve a functional purpose: they keep the cat warm. Photo by Louise Van der Meid.

Going formal, these two winners owned by Mrs. Fred Galvin are: (left) TR. GR. AND QUAD. CH. FAN-T-CEE'S ENCHANTRESS and (right) TR. GR. AND QUAD. CH. FAN-T-CEE'S KABAR KENNY. Photo by VIctor Baldwin.

There are little poodle pants available in pet stores, very useful for a female cat in season, as sometimes they will "spray," the same as a male does. We put these poodle pants on our unaltered males when we want to let them out of their cages, where they usually are confined because of their spraying habit (explained in Chapter XI). We let them out one at a time to run, visit with us, and play with the other cats and kittens, all of which they enjoy. These pants take a bit of getting used to on the part of the cat, but if he is induced to forget about the pants and chase a ball or another cat, he soon forgets all about them, providing they are not too tight.

Anyone who knows how to sew could make all sorts of clothes for a cat. One southern California breeder, Peggy Galvin, is gifted along this line and has made some very attractive sets for cats. I purchased a tuxedo for one of my male cats, and for one of my females a set consisting of a painted basket decorated with pink glazed chintz, with a pillow to match, both reversible, of a different shade of pink on each side. There was a matching reversible sweater and jeweled leash—and, for good measure, a little pink mouse.

Cat Clothes for People

Two other southern California breeders, Barbara Layton and Dorothy Bond, custom-make sweaters for humans. I have a light blue sweater that Barbara made, with two Siamese on the front and, on the back, kittens with their backs toward the viewer. We ordered a sweater of the same color for my husband, with a lovely Blue Point featured on the front, and Dorothy made him a pair of socks to match, complete to Blue Points.

Another breeder, in the San Francisco area, Esther Illingsworth, makes unusual Siamese jewelry, ash trays, pins, mugs, and so on. I have a pair of Blue Point earrings and a Blue Point pin that I wear only occasionally because I am afraid something will happen to them. Esther made me a striking television lamp, copying from a photograph of two of our show cats. This is so priceless to me that I don't use it, either, because I just know it would get broken if I should.

It is fun trying to find Siamese-cat Christmas cards to send, although sometimes it is fruitless. Some years I have had to give up and have them made from photographs of my own cats.

CHAPTER VII

GROOMING

Coat

You should brush your cat's coat every day. However, being human, we let it go sometimes, possibly for weeks. One of the advantages of owning a Siamese cat is that no great harm will be done if you do let the daily brushing go. Of course, you should brush the dead hair out of his coat periodically, as otherwise he will get an excess of hair in his stomach from licking himself continually, as all cats do. While it is possible for Siamese cats to get hair balls, it is rather rare—and absolutely unnecessary. The best brush for Siamese coats is the hard rubber brush purchased only at pet stores. Brush your cat with it, and you will hardly believe how much dead hair will come out of his coat.

My introduction to a rubber brush was at a cat show. A well-known Midwestern breeder had looked me up, and I was flattered. My cat was due to go up to be judged, so I took him out of his cage and started the usual last-minute wipedown with a chamois. Apparently, my new acquaintance noticed much dead hair in the cat's coat. She asked me if I had a rubber brush, and I had to say that I did not. She told me to go borrow one and she would show me something. I quickly borrowed a rubber brush and handed it to her. I was embarrassed at the amount of dead hair that came out of that cat's coat! I filled a whole pan with it. And I had thought he was in show condition! I had religiously brushed him with an ordinary bristle brush. Needless to say, I have used none but the rubber brush since.

However, a word of caution: use the rubber brush with care; brush only enough to get out the dead hair. If you continue brushing you will be pulling out live hair, which will grow back dark, and you will be wondering what happened to the cat's coat. So, while I heartily recommend using a rubber brush, use it cautiously. Finish off the grooming with your bare hands. Stroke the cat repeatedly to get off the final hairs the brush has loosened. If you dampen your hands first, you will be able to get all the loose hairs off. The more you stroke him, the more the coat will shine. Cats like to be groomed. When I start on my older cats that are used to being brushed, they sit right down and enjoy it, as shown by their actions and their loud purring.

Bathing

Occasionally, you may want to bathe your cat, although Siamese never really need a bath. The only time I ever bathe a cat is when a male being used at stud gets to feeling sticky or gritty, or possibly a little too smelly. A dry shampoo may be used when you don't want to give a full bath. Some owners "touch up" their cat with a dry shampoo before, or during, a show. Breeders of Frost Points and Chocolate Points bathe their cats several days before a show so the natural oils will have time to return to give these light-colored coats their beautiful sheen.

You will find many shampoos at pet stores. Choose one that specifically says "for cats" on the label. Cats cannot always take the same preparations as dogs, so I never choose those that read "for dogs and cats."

Get all the things you will need for the bath together where you can reach them, but place them out of reach of a struggling cat. The best plan is to have someone help you. One person holds the cat's front legs with one hand and the hind legs with the other, while the other person lathers and rinses the cat. The trick is to work fast. Don't ever put the cat's head under water, and don't get soap in his eyes or mouth. We stand the cat up in the sink and run in the water, we soap him well all over, run the wash water out and the rinse water in, making sure at all times that the water is tepid. The person holding

Dry bath products are useful in cleaning the cat at times when it needs cleaning short of a full bath. Photo by Louise Van der Meid.

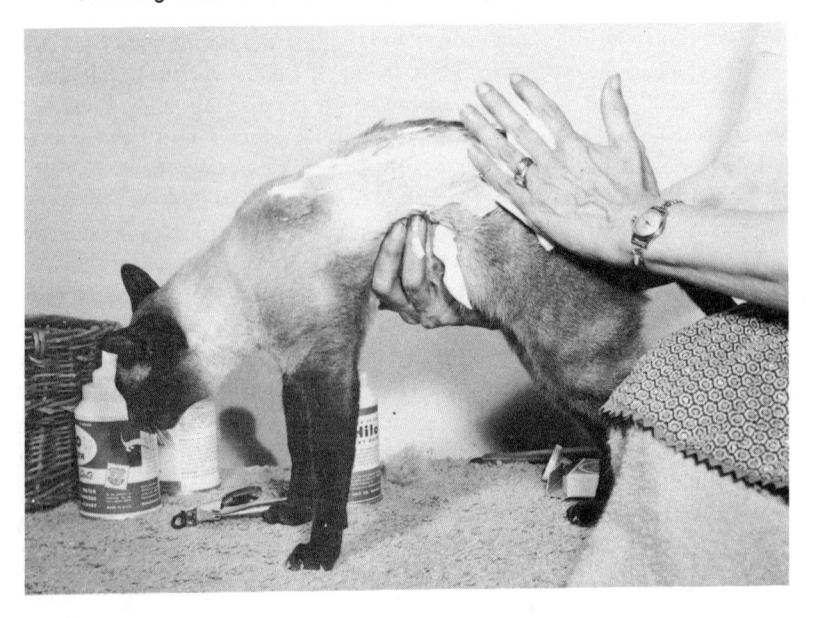

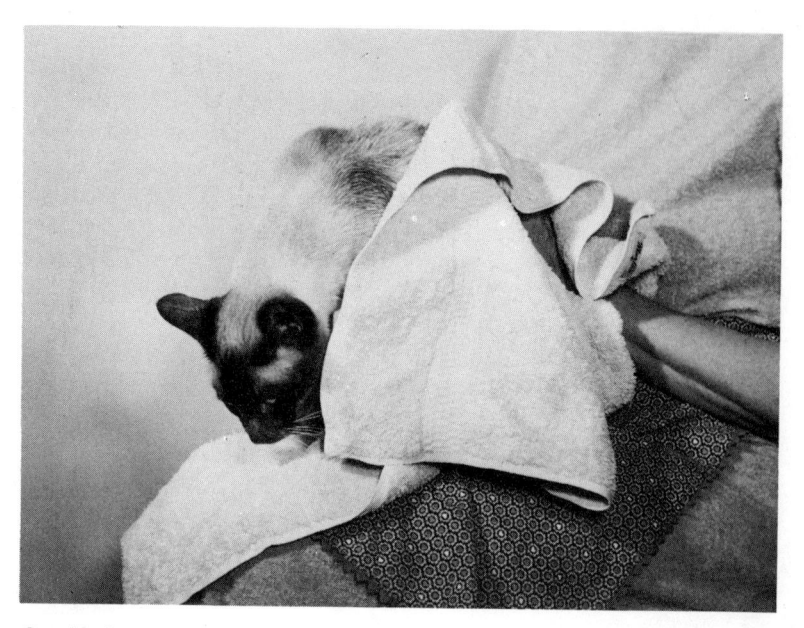

On the few occasions when a bath might be necessary, make sure that the cat is dried well afterward to prevent contraction of respiratory infections. Photo by Louise Van der Meid.

him can then quickly turn him upside down while the one washing rinses the cat's back. Be sure to rinse all soap out of the coat. Rinse until the hair "squeaks." I like to have a "people" rinse ready to pour over the cat just before he comes out of the water. This leaves his coat soft, manageable, and fragrant.

Transfer the cat quickly to a big towel. Fold it around him with his head outside, and rub and rub to get the water out of his coat. The towel soon will become too wet, so have another one handy to finish up the job. If it is a warm sunny day, take him out in the sunshine to finish drying. Take along his flea comb and comb the wet fur into place with it. The fine teeth will lay it down just where you want it while removing any fleas that might be in it. If it is cold outdoors, finish drying the cat in a warm room. Don't let him get in any drafts or get cold in any way for the rest of the day. After you have finished with him, the cat of course will wash himself all over again. (After all, you got him "dirty," you know!) But, when it is all finished, he will be clean, happy, and proud.

Claws

When kept indoors, his claws grow very sharp. Pet stores have nail clippers

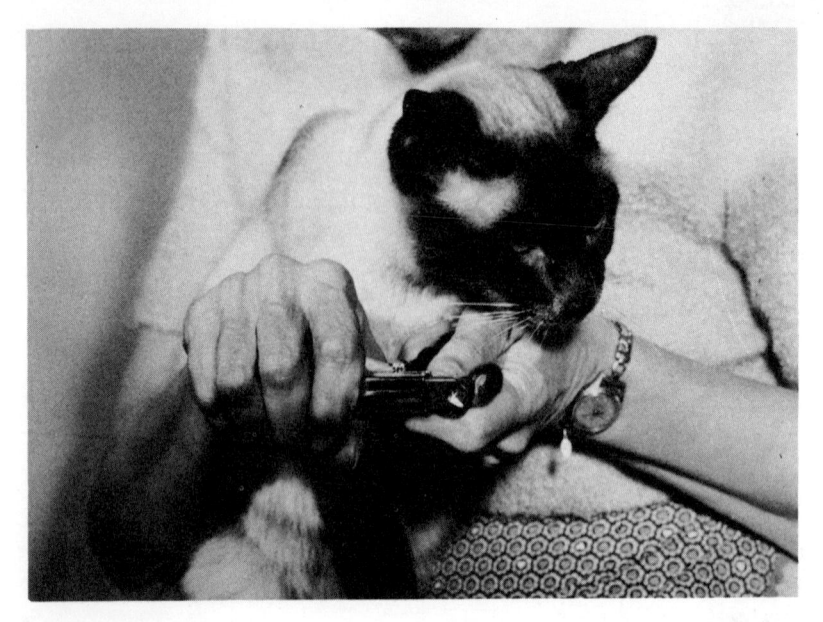

In clipping your cat's claws, use only those clippers designed specifically for use on cats, which make the job easier and safer. Photo by Louise Van der Meid.

for sale. Buy a pair and nip off the tip ends of the claws only. Be very careful not to get into the "quick." Do this often, perhaps once a week. This way, a cat's claws aren't so sharp that they continually catch in things, and you aren't accidently scratched when he is playing with you. The scratching pole helps to keep claws rounded off, too. Claws on the hind feet will not need clipping as often as those on forepaws, as they tend to wear off more than those on the front paws.

Ears

Some cats have a dark wax in their ears. This looks rather like ear mites to anyone who doesn't know much about cats. It can, and should be, cleaned out easily. Dip a "Q" tip in a bit of oil. Work it carefully in the many crevices of the cat's ear, being careful not to get too deep into the ear and harming the eardrum. The cat won't care for this treatment, but he will look much better. (For treatment of ear mites, see Chapter IX.)

Eyes

Often a cat will have a bit of a discharge from his eyes that will crust or

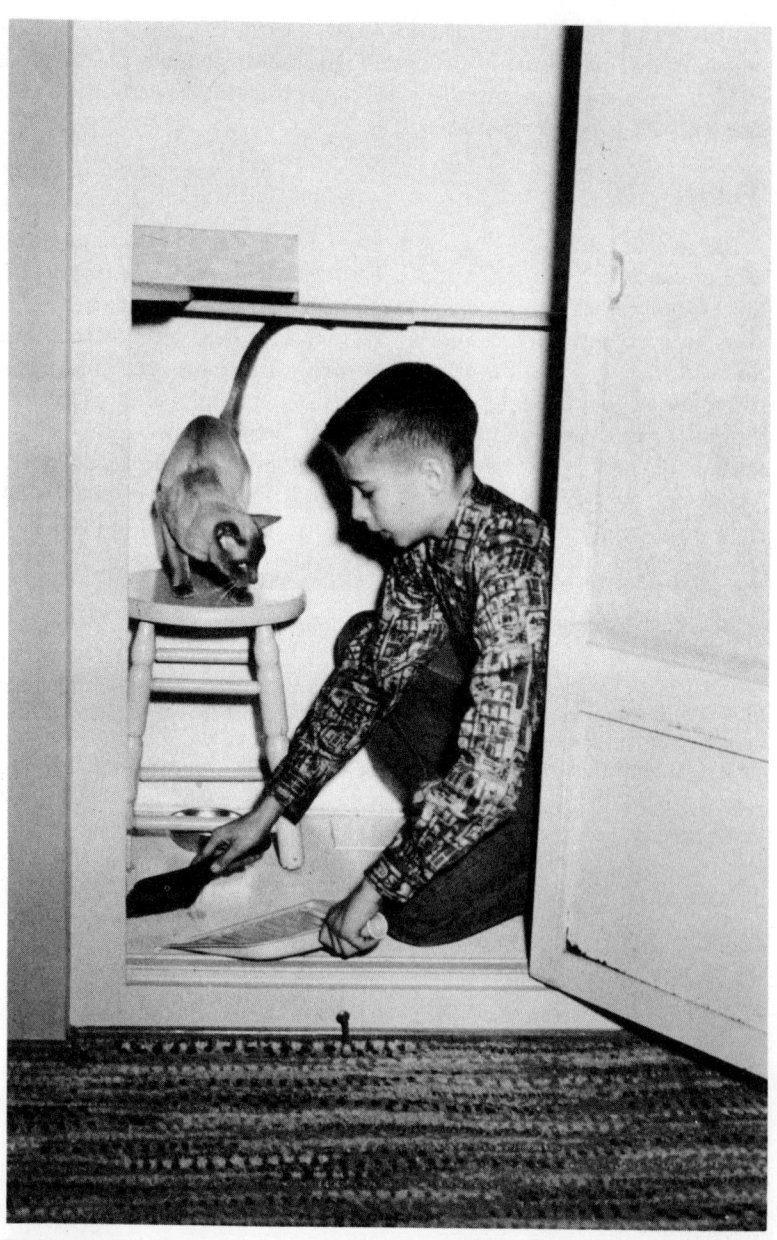

Dirt is the breeding ground of disease. This young owner knows this and keeps his cat's quarters clean at all times. Photo by Louise Van der Meid.

harden during the night, just as with our own eyes. Take a soft piece of tissue and clean this out. Usually, it is nothing to concern you, but the cat presents a much better appearance if it is wiped away. If discharge becomes excessive, check it with your veterinarian.

Teeth

I have read articles on cleaning a cat's teeth with a toothbrush and soda to take the tartar off. No doubt this is entirely within the realm of possibility, but I would rather control this problem with diet. Give the cat some bones to chew on every few days, as this is how they keep their teeth in condition in the wild state, and it still works quite well for the domesticated cat. Be sure the bones are sturdy enough so they won't splinter and a sharp piece stick in the mouth or throat, and be sure they are large enough so the cat won't swallow the bone, yet small enough so he can give his teeth a good workout. There are many dry-food products on the market that are good for a cat to chew on to keep his teeth clean. (See Chapter VIII.)

Fleas

I think there is nothing more cruel than to allow any animal to become

Blue Point female owned by Grace Forrest and Jean and Bill Quiner, bred by Mrs. Fred Galvin: CH. FAN-T-CEE FLYCKA OF BOGRAE. Sire: DiNapoli's Duke of Fan-T-Cee; dam: Fan-T-Cee's Blue Rose.

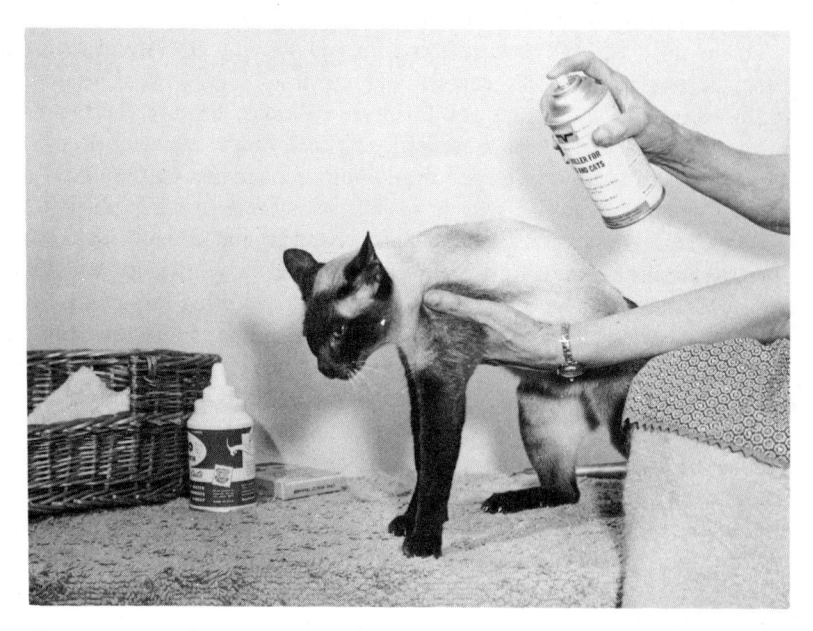

Fleas are troublesome and dangerous; luckily, they can be safeguarded against by the use of special flea preparations available from your pet dealer. Photo by Louise Van der Meid.

infested with fleas and scratch continually. A cat should not have *one* flea on him, ever. Besides, fleas are the intermediate host of the cat tapeworm. In other words, it is from fleas that your cat gets tapeworms. (We will discuss getting rid of tapeworms in Chapter IX.)

Cat fleas are small and dark brown or black in color. Dog fleas are larger and a lighter brown in color. All kinds of fleas will bite and live off the blood of any animal, including humans. Fleas bite some people eagerly, but seldom bother others. Some cats seem to attract more fleas than others of the same breed. Cat fleas prefer to bite cats, but if your animals are away from the house for a few days, the fleas will become hungry and bite you instead. Before their animals are brought back from wherever they were boarded or kept, many people returning from a vacation notice for the first time that there are fleas in their houses. With persistent effort, fleas can be eliminated completely from a house cat, if he is always kept indoors and is not exposed to reinfestation. But if you have a dog or cat that runs loose, it will bring fleas into your house. Sometimes fleas will ride into the house on your socks or clothing without your being aware of their presence. Flea eggs drop off an animal and the larvae hatch in various places around the house. They enter the pupal stage and later emerge as an adult flea that will jump on the animal.

This is a vicious circle. The fleas must be exterminated.

To do this, wash all washable articles and vacuum floors and furniture often, particularly in dark corners and crevices. Flea powder should be sprinkled on and under rugs and furniture cushions. Be sure you use a flea powder that is a product made especially for cats. Preparations for dogs could kill your cat. Recently developed flea-killing preparations that are non-toxic to cats contain four to five percent malathion as the active ingredient to be effective. Malathion is safe for limited use on and around kittens. It also can be purchased in liquid form from a nursery for use in spraying your yard. Other flea-control products work on the principle of dehydrating the insect. These claim long-lasting effectiveness, particularly in furniture and sleeping places.

Evidence of adult fleas on a cat are grains of "flea dirt" (excrement) on his skin and throughout the coat. This is a black gritty-feeling substance which turns red when wet. The eggs are white and too small for ordinary notice. The larvae are small, with thirteen pairs of legs, and resemble a very tiny centipede. Check your cat and kittens often for signs of fleas. Severe flea infestation on a kitten or cat can cause anemia and even death. Fleas can severely drain the blood supply and weaken the system of a cat or any animal. A small amount of flea powder on the back of the neck, under the chin, and at the base of the tail, applied daily for ten days or two weeks, should rid your cat of adult fleas. Follow-up with a biweekly application of flea powder and house cleaning until you are sure there are no more fleas in any stage. After that, keep the flea problem under control with a flea comb purchased from your pet store. Be sure to buy a flea comb with very fine teeth; otherwise, you might as well not have one. Comb through your cat's fur each day and catch any fleas that might have jumped on him from anywhere. You may find one or two, but this is hardly a problem, especially if you kill these so they won't multiply.

There is a flea collar on the market that is good to put on cats that run loose. The principle of this collar is that a bit of powder is let out on the skin of the neck as the cat moves. Since fleas move actively about, they eventually pass along the cat's neck and make contact with the flea collar. You will find many spray-type flea killers on the market today.

To kill a flea you have raked out of your cat's coat with a flea comb, or caught by any method, roll him tightly between your thumb and forefinger to stun him, allowing you to drop him onto a tissue and crack him with your thumb. If you have a bit of hair from the cat lying on the tissue and drop the partially stunned flea into the hair, it will snare him until you can kill him. If the flea comes to and starts jumping, you'll be lucky to catch him again.

De-Clawing

De-clawing is believed by many to be the answer to the upholstery-

Seal Point female owned and bred by Carlon Boren: R.M. DBL. GRAND AND QUAD. CH. BOREN'S TWEETER. Sire: Boren's Luck-E-Boy II; dam: Boren's Ku Do.

Blue Point male owned by Mrs. Irving Cromarty, bred by Mrs. Fred Galvin: QUAD. CH. FAN-T-CEE'S FAUN OF CROM-ARTY. Sire: Kabar Alexander the Great; dam: Fan-T-Cee's Dee Dee.

scratching problem arising from having a cat. Many more who love cats frown on this practice. A de-clawed cat can never be entered in a show. If you are considering taking your pet's major defense away from him permanently, please first weigh carefully the following consequences:

Major surgery under complete anesthesia (always a risk) is required to accomplish de-clawing without mutilation. If the operation is done improperly, it will cause your cat great pain and misery.

I am sorry to have to tell you that there are veterinarians who will inform you there is nothing to the operation. They will not take the time, effort, or patience to do it properly. There are those that simply jerk the claws out. You will find yourself looking up another veterinarian to repair the damage the first has done, which will be expensive—to say nothing of the excruciating pain your cat must endure.

Have you ever considered what might happen to your loved one if he ever gets outside by accident? If he were to get into a fight with another cat, he would be unmercifully cut up by the other cat's claws, having none of his own to defend himself with.

If anything ever happened that you had to give up your cat, how could you be sure that the person who got him would be careful not to ever let him out? If you must de-claw your cat and then find that you have to give him up, please have your veterinarian put him to sleep. This is the only way to be sure he won't be subjected to cruel maulings by other animals.

Also, if you must have your cat de-clawed, have just the front paws done. This still leaves him some protection, as they learn to climb with their hind feet and, of course, they always fight with their hind feet.

I am sure many persons will not agree with me, but I just cannot see how any piece of furniture ever could be more important to me than my cats, especially when they can be trained to use nothing but their scratching posts.

CHAPTER VIII
FEEDING CATS AND KITTENS

Kittens

The mother cat takes complete care of the kittens until they are four weeks old. We like to start our kits on a mixture of Pablum, canned milk, powdered vitamin, and egg yolk, mixed together with enough boiling water to make a soft, almost runny, consistency. The boiling water warms the mixture just enough. For the kittens' very first meal, at about four weeks of age, I mix the above ingredients on a flat dish and then sit down with the kits, taking each one and placing a bit of the food on the tip of his nose. Naturally, he licks it

Chocolate Point male owned by Mrs. Wreatha Dellinger, bred by Mrs. Helen Koscak; TR. CH. KOSCAK'S CHOCO KEO OF BLUE MASK. Sire: Koscak's Suki; dam: Dawshome Yolashke (Imp.) Photo by Mary Lucille Carothers.

Blue Point male bred and owned by Marge Naples: DBL. GR. AND QUAD. CH. DiNAPOLI'S SERENADE IN BLUE. Sire: Ta-Lee-Ho's Al-La-Bi; dam: DiNapoli's Phet. Photo by Victor Baldwin.

Chocolate Point female owned and bred by Mrs. Helen C. Koscak: GR. AND QUAD. CH. KOSCAK'S CHOCO-VIXEN. Sire: Koscak's Suki; dam: Dawshome Yolashka (Imp.). Photo by Gordon Laughner.

off and finds it tastes pretty good. By this time, I have some more on the tip of my finger, and he soon licks this off. Then I take another bit on my finger, and as he licks it, I gradually bring the finger down to the plate. First thing you know, the kit is licking the food off the plate. Pile the mixture up right around the sides of the plate.

Don't be discouraged if they don't get this routine the first time, or even if they do that they won't go for it sometimes the next time. After a few days they are screaming for their dinner when they see you coming with the plate. Of course, the sooner you get them onto food, the sooner you get the increasing load off the mother. They will still nurse, but they won't require as much of her milk.

If you can keep the little ones on this diet for a couple of weeks, you are doing very well. They usually get into their mother's plate of meat long before that, and once they have tasted meat, of course they prefer it. Watch carefully; sometimes there will be a kitten allergic to egg yolk. He will throw up his food, and you won't offer it again to that particular kitten. The mother cat will eat this Pablum mixture, too, to show the kittens how it is done. It is

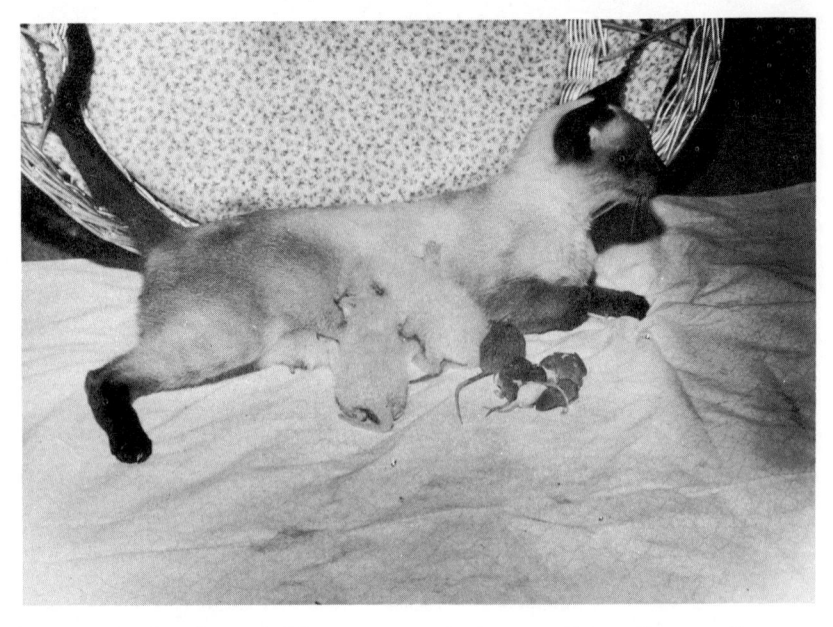

Cats and other household pets can get along well together, as they are not sworn enemies from birth. This nursing Siamese mother proves the point by being oblivious of the family of mice nestled near her.

good for her. We have had litters of kittens that started sampling mother's food before I got them started on Pablum, and then there was no use bothering with it at all. These kits have gotten along just as well as those started on Pablum. I simply mixed the mother's meat to a little more moist consistency and put down enough for her and the kits. Little kittens should be fed four or five times a day.

Vitamins

Siamese cats must always be given vitamins. Any good multiple product should serve nicely. These come in syrup or dry form. With one or two cats, we used to give them their vitamins from a spoon, which they licked clean. However, with multiple cats, it is much easier to mix a dry vitamin product into their food. The make-up of a Siamese cat appears to require supplementation of vitamin A. Growing kittens, pregnant and nursing mothers, especially, need calcium, which cannot be adequately assimilated without vitamin D. There are many products on the market that combine calcium and vitamin D. However, a little cod liver oil given with calcium will accomplish the same thing. I have been told that dry yeast, which many people like to give their cats, darkens the Siamese cat's coat.

Frost Point male owned and bred by Mrs. Edwin Berger: GR. & QUAD. CH. JUDO'S JACK FROST. Sire: Ta-Lee-Ho's Al-La-Bi; dam: Mi-Lana of Judo. Photo by Gordon Jarvis.

Beware of "hair-growing" preparations. These are for Persian cats. Part of a Siamese cat's beauty is his short, close coat, which will naturally be sleek and glossy if the cat is in good health and you keep the dead hair brushed out. A judge once told me that vitamin B tends to grow "plushy" coats on Siamese cats. Therefore, I try to choose multiple vitamin products that do not overly stress the B vitamins. I am not saying Siamese cats do not need vitamin B: I definitely believe they do, but I don't think they need the products that have an over-abundance of the various B vitamins.

A Diet for Siamese

All cats are basically carnivorous, and their diet should consist of a great deal of meat. In the wild state, they ate small animals and birds; it follows, then, that raw meats and such things as liver, heart, kidney, and melts are good for cats. I have a strong conviction that Siamese cats require a different diet from other breeds of cats. Since Siamese are the only breed I have raised, I cannot prove my theory. Many books on Siamese tell us that their systems cannot assimilate fat. On the other hand, veterinarians, breeders, and judges all feel cats need about 25% fat in their diet. I have always avoided adding

Food should be fed in a low pan, as Siamese have an aversion to placing their heads into steep containers. Photo by Louise Van der Meid.

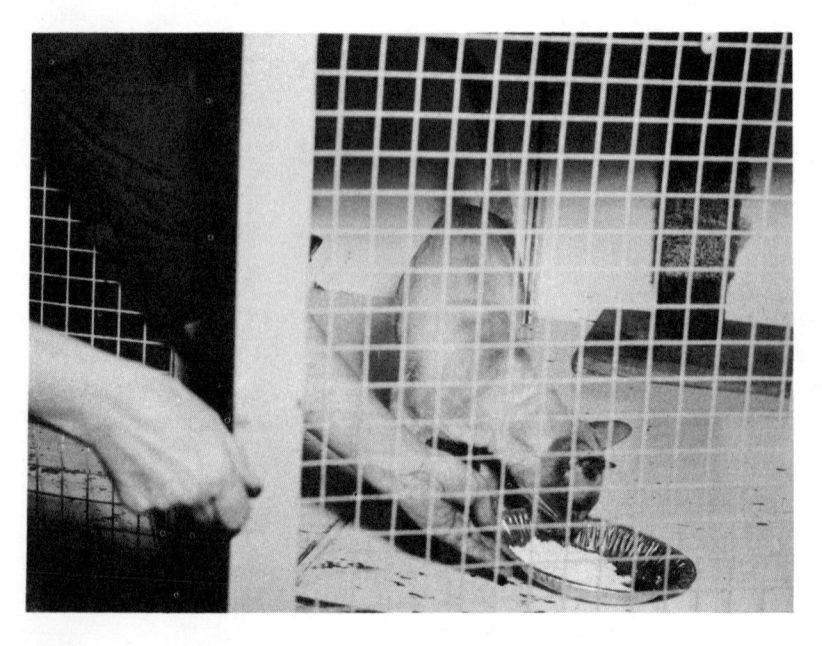

Blue Point female bred and owned by Mrs. Fred Galvin: QUAD. GR. AND QUINT. CH. FAN-T-CEE'S BLUE FANCY. Sire: Ta-Lee-Ho's Al-La-Bi; dam: Kabar's Miss Fancy of Fan-T-Cee. Photo by Victor Baldwin.

Blue Point male owned and bred by Marge and John Naples: TR. GR. AND QUAD. CH. DiNAPOLI'S BLUE TANGO. Sire: Fan-T-Cee's Tee Cee; dam: DiNapoli's Phet. Photo by Victor Baldwin.

fats to my cats' diet, except for a tablespoonful of cooking oil, preferably soy bean oil, in their food once a week.

Some people prefer to feed beef as the cat's basic food. We have always fed horsemeat. While some breeders feel horsemeat contains too much acid for a steady diet, we have fed it for several years and have had no digestive problems. To prepare my cats' food, I start by boiling some water. While it is coming to a boil, I put into a bowl one pound of coarse-ground horsemeat, one-half a tall can of a good canned food, some dry kibble or meal, sufficient powdered vitamins for the number of cats I am feeding, some garlic salt (because this mixture strikes me as being rather tasteless), and then pour sufficient boiling water over the ingredients to make a soft consistency when all mixed together. This boiling water takes the chill off the refrigerated meat but does not cook it. Anything right out of the refrigerator is too cold for a cat's stomach. To the mixture may be added egg yolk, if desired, but don't put in the egg white. This is another thing a cat's system cannot assimilate, and too much albumen is detrimental. At times I add some powdered milk, as we never give our cats milk in any other form. I usually have some small cans of kidney, liver, and chicken on hand to use if I forget to put the horsemeat out to thaw, and to give kittens a midday meal or midnight snack.

Occasionally, we vary this diet by treating the cats to a meal of baked fresh fish, flaked off the bones. They relish this for one meal, but refuse it if offered for the next. Besides, I find that it tends to cause loose stools.

Milk

Contrary to popular opinion, cats do not require milk as a permanent part of their diet. It often causes loose bowels. If you notice your cat is constipated, you can alleviate the situation by giving him milk. If his bowels become too loose, take him off milk entirely and feed him only solids such as the canned foods containing cereals. If you feel he should have milk, a mixture of half canned milk and half water is preferable.

Water

Cats should always have fresh water. Usually they prefer to drink it directly from the faucet as it drips, or from a dish standing in the sink with water in it, or from a vase or flat dish with an arrangement of flowers in it!

In a cattery housing a number of cats, the preparation of meals must be done on a businesslike basis to assure that all cats get just the right amount of nutritious food necessary for good health and good looks. Photo by Louise Van der Meid.

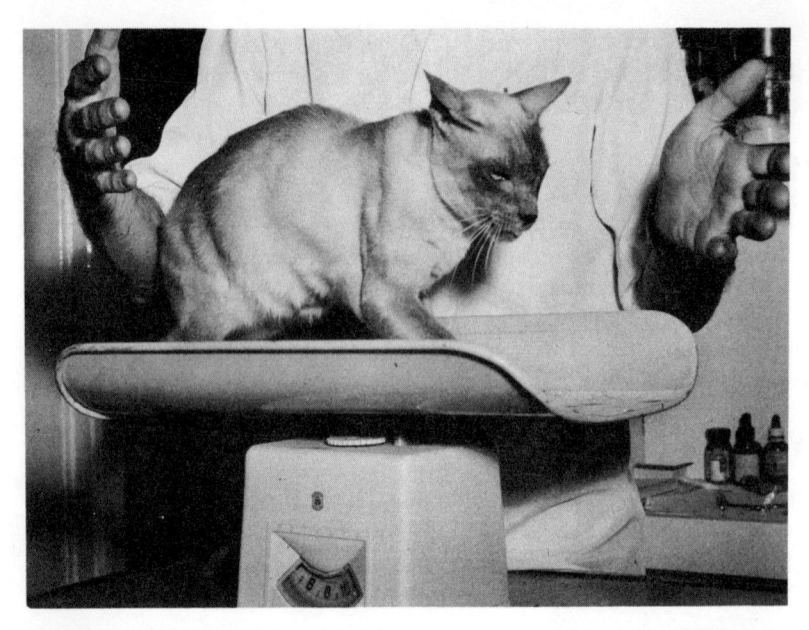

Both obesity and thinness detract from the appearance of your Siamese, so keep a close check on your cat's weight and general proportions. Photo by Louise Van der Meid.

Food From Your Table

It is quite all right to feed your cat anything you wish from your table, but don't feel that he is getting a well-balanced diet from this fare. He may eat some vegetables, but he will never get a sufficient quantity to supplant his need for multiple vitamins. You may find he likes such strange things as cantaloupe, avocado, corn on the cob, or beets. He will love butter and crisp fried bacon. Any of these things can be a treat for a cat, but should not replace his regular food.

If you go off somewhere leaving your table uncleared, and the cat gets up and helps himself, don't punish the cat. He is only doing what comes naturally. Wouldn't it be better to take all the things you don't want him to sample from the table or sink before you leave the room? This would keep you on your toes, too. Who is teaching whom?

Quantity of Food

Each cat has his own individual requirements as to quantity of food. They should be fed twice a day. Kittens, of course, need to eat often, and nursing cats need generous portions, and perhaps even three meals a day. Cats are a great deal like human beings. Some are built hefty, and these cats need only a rounded tablespoonful or so of food twice a day. You are never doing a cat a favor by overfeeding him. You could kill him this way. Other cats are naturally lean and lithe. These cats actually need more food than their stocky cousins to maintain a sufficient amount of fat. If you can feel a cat's backbone when you stroke him, he is too thin. A fat Siamese cat has lost a great deal of his natural beauty, and liveliness as well. If your cat runs loose, usually someone will feed him, and you will never know what he is getting, or how much.

Occasionally a cat will need a special diet. If yours isn't doing well on what you are feeding him, consult your veterinarian, who may prescribe a special diet. He may also stock specially prepared diets in cans which may be purchased individually or by the case.

How to Feed

A cat should be fed on a flat dish or paper. He dislikes putting his head and muzzle into a container. If his food is spread out on a flat dish, he will take longer to eat it, thus controlling any tendency to gulp. Each meal should be fed on a clean plate. When the dish has been down about fifteen minutes, it

Seal Point male owned by Mr. and Mrs. Dan Vellinga, bred by Mrs. Kathleen Williams of England: R.M. TR. CH. DONERAILE SABU OF PANDARA (IMP.) Sire: Doneraile Druid; dam: Tia Mie Trinket.

should be taken up, even if the food has not been eaten. If your cat becomes a "finicky" eater, you are spoiling him, and have only yourself to blame. If you have one cat, it is hard not to pamper him, but he is better off if you don't. If the cat does not eat what you offer him, take it away. Probably next time he is fed he will be eager to eat.

What Not to Feed

Chicken bones should never be given to a cat, because they splinter easily. A cat could get one of these splinters caught in his throat and choke on it. The meat of a chicken, however, is very good for a cat, and they love it.

Fish contains thiaminase which destroys vitamin B_1, or thiamin. Red meat tuna is very well liked by some cats, but must not be used as an exclusive diet. There have been cases where a vitamin E deficiency disease called "yellow fat disease" has caused the death of cats whose diets were largely, or entirely, red meat tuna. Most manufacturers have now added the vitamin E to their products, but it is still advisable not to let it be your cat's main food. Fish, chicken, and pork bones all splinter easily and should not be given to a cat to chew on. Also, beware of any source of ground pet meat that has neckbone or any kind of bone ground up with the meat. These minute pieces of bone could be swallowed without being chewed and it is possible that they could lodge in the intestines and cause trouble.

Pork is not a good meat for a cat's diet. If served at all, be sure it is well cooked.

CHAPTER IX

HEALTH OF YOUR KITTENS AND CATS

This chapter is by no means meant to alarm you, but for the new owner a little knowledge may mean the difference between life and death for his cat.

Veterinarian

Find yourself a good veterinarian in whom you have faith. Try to find one who owns and likes cats. If you visit him regularly, your veterinarian won't mind your calling occasionally just for advice. He may come to feel that you are capable of giving simple medication yourself, in which case he will sell you the required medication and instruct you on its use. A cat is always much happier at home with you when he is sick, if it is at all possible for you to care for him.

Blue Point male owned by Mrs. Harriet Wolfgang: CH. ERICKSON'S HERR WOLFGANG. Sire: Ch. Wolfgang's Von Baron; dam: Wolfgang's Fanci Malane.

135

Lilac Point male owned by Eloise and Frank Magnan: GR. AND QUINT. CH. RED WING'S CHO-ABI OF ELO-YSE. Sire: Elo-yse's Choc-Abi of El Rancho; dam: Red Wing's Blue Fluer. Bred by Nina Ferguson.

Is Your Cat Sick?

It is natural for a cat to be in good health. If you keep your cat inside, many of the following ailments can be avoided. You will readily notice if he is not acting right, and he will avoid contact with the contagious diseases, for the most part.

One of the first signs that your cat is a bit under the weather is his lack of appetite. Another sign of trouble is loose bowels. If you notice your cat has what looks like a film covering part of his eyes, this is the third eyelid, or haw, which ordinarily covers his eyes only when he is sleeping. If this haw continues to cover part of his eye, something is wrong. Another reliable sign that all is not well is for the cat's coat to become tacky. His fur will lose its luster and stand away from his body. If your cat sleeps or drowses in a "hunched up" position and does not respond to your touch or call, he is not feeling well. Your cat is usually alert and watches any moving thing. If you find him just staring into space, something is wrong. Sometimes the cause is simple. If he does not respond quickly to the suggested remedies for minor ailments, consult your veterinarian immediately. In good faith and ignorance, you can do great harm by treating him yourself, because so many illnesses are

Blue Point Siamese (left), Seal Point Siamese (right)
Photo by Louise Van der Meid.

Siamese regularly take time out from their frolicking for a little human companionship. Photo by Louise Van der Meid.

Dry shampoos are useful for touching up a Siamese before a show and when the cat is just dirty enough to require some type of cleansing, but not necessarily a full bath. Photo by Louise Van der Meid.

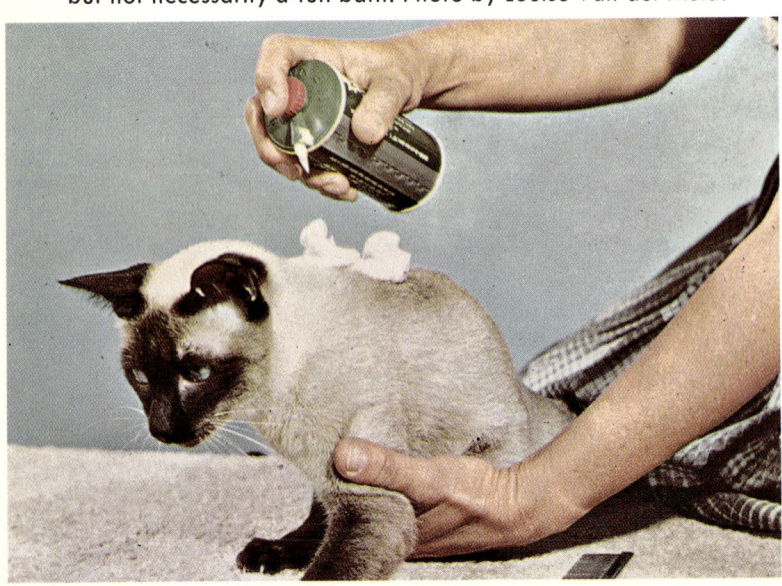

Seal Point female owned and bred by Lillian Pedulla: DBL. GR. CH. CYMRI DEE-VA. Sire: Cymri Cri-Ket; dam: LaCores Jennifer.

closely related and have similar symptoms. The cheapest life insurance for your pet is to avail yourself of your veterinarian's experience and skill promptly if anything seems abnormal. In the past twenty years veterinary diagnosis and treatment have advanced greatly. There is a broad range of drugs available which are generally manufactured under the same exacting conditions and specifications as those for human use. Surgery of the most delicate nature is performed, such as setting and pinning broken bones, Caesarian section and other abdominal surgery, and eye and chest surgery. All are performed using aseptic methods and improved anesthesia. All of these increase the chances for successful surgery.

How to Give a Pill or Capsule

If you are right-handed, hold the cat's head in your left hand, open the cat's mouth with the index or little finger of the right hand, and hold it open with the thumb and longest finger of the left hand. You will note a little groove formed at the base of the tongue. Drop the pill or capsule into this groove and give it a push into the throat with the index finger of your right hand. Transfer your left hand to the nape of the cat's neck and pull his head

Blue Point female owned by Mrs. Marjorie Elliott, bred by Karen Burt: QUAD. CH. SKY HILL'S SKI-LO OF SHAN LING. Photo by "Muzzie."

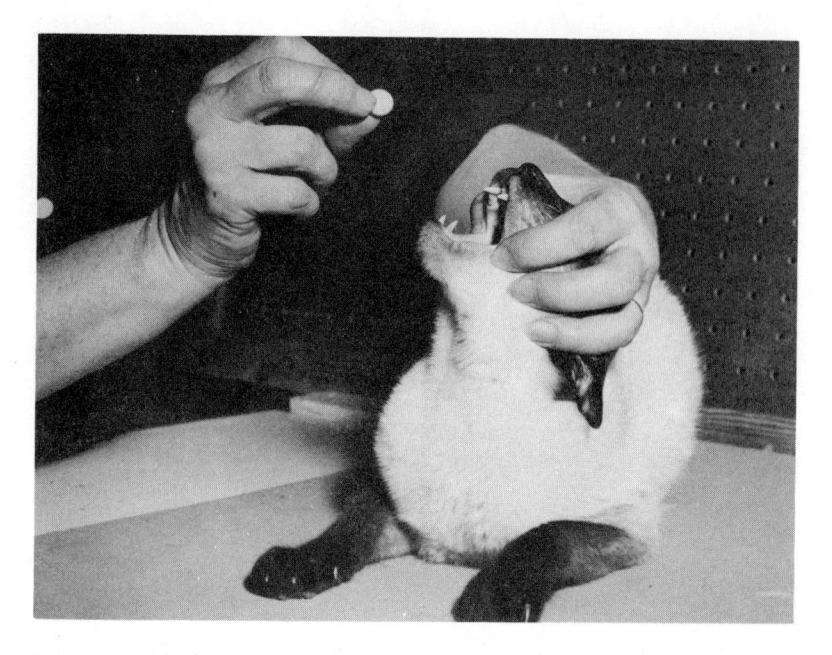

Feeding the cat a pill the right way takes a little practice, but eventually the trick is mastered. Photo by Louise Van der Meid.

right back while supporting his back and his hind legs with your right hand until he is upside down. If all this is done quickly, he will be so surprised he will swallow the pill before he knows what has happened. Sometimes it is easier to pull this trick if you are sitting down holding the cat in your lap. If he succeeds in spitting the pill out, hold him and pet him awhile, then try again. In the case of capsules, it is helpful if you coat the capsule with a bit of butter just before you give it. This will serve as lubrication, and the capsule will go down much more easily.

How to Give Liquid Medication

Most bottles containing liquid medicine have a plastic, rather than glass, medicine dropper as part of the cap. This is a great improvement. A cat will often try to bite a dropper; if it is glass, he could easily crush it and end up swallowing fine bits of glass, which would be disastrous. They seldom harm the tough plastic. These droppers can be boiled and kept in a clean place for future use.

To give the liquid medication, fill the dropper with the desired amount of medicine, grasp the cat's head with the left hand in the same manner you would for giving a pill, and hold the mouth open a little way. With the right hand, insert the dropper at the side of the mouth and let the medicine flow

This orphaned kitten is being cared for by being fed from an eye dropper. A plastic dropper is much preferred over a glass dropper in feeding kittens and administering liquid medication. Photo by Victor Baldwin.

slowly out of the dropper onto the cat's tongue. He has no choice other than to swallow the medicine. If the cat finds the medicine distasteful, he will allow as much of the medicine as possible to drip out of the corners of his mouth. Have a tissue handy and wipe the mouth until it is clean, while still holding the cat's head; otherwise, he will shake his head and the medicine will fly in all directions.

How to Take a Cat's Temperature

If your cat is sick it is helpful to take his temperature before taking him to the veterinarian, for often his temperature will shoot up when he finds he is in the veterinarian's office. I have a cat that we came entirely too close to losing when he was about a year old, and he has never forgotten his trips to the veterinarian. If I take him in now, even though it is a different building and a different veterinarian, the minute I open the door to go in he begins frothing at the mouth.

Seal Point female owned and bred by Mrs. Fred Galvin: TR. GR. AND QUINT. CH. FAN-T-CEE'S ENCHANTRESS. Sire: Kabar's Alexander the Great; dam: Fan-T-Cee's Fatima. Photo by Victor Baldwin.

You should have a rectal thermometer at home for taking a cat's temperature. Lubricate the thermometer with some white vaseline. Grasp the cat's tail at the base with your left hand while holding him against your side with your arm, and gently insert the thermometer in the rectum to a distance of approximately two inches. Leave the thermometer inserted for about two minutes, holding the cat to keep him quiet. When you remove the thermometer, read the temperature before cleaning it. A cat's normal temperature is 101.5°. Clean the thermometer with a piece of cotton moistened with alcohol, shake it down below 95°, and put it away. If a cat's temperature remains below or above normal for more than a day, something is wrong.

If you do not have a thermometer, but your cat's body feels warmer than usual, and his paw and nose leather and his ears are very warm to your touch, he no doubt has a high temperature. He will also be listless and quiet. If a cat has a temperature, his body is fighting an infection. However, even worse than running a temperature is for a cat to have a subnormal temperature. If you think your cat is sick, and he feels cold when you touch him, lose no time in getting him to your veterinarian.

Seal Point male owned and bred by Barbara Layton: DBL. GR. AND QUAD. CH. MOONTIDE DIMMER. Sire: Palos Verdes Avatar; dam: Quinn's Misty Blue. Photo by Layton.

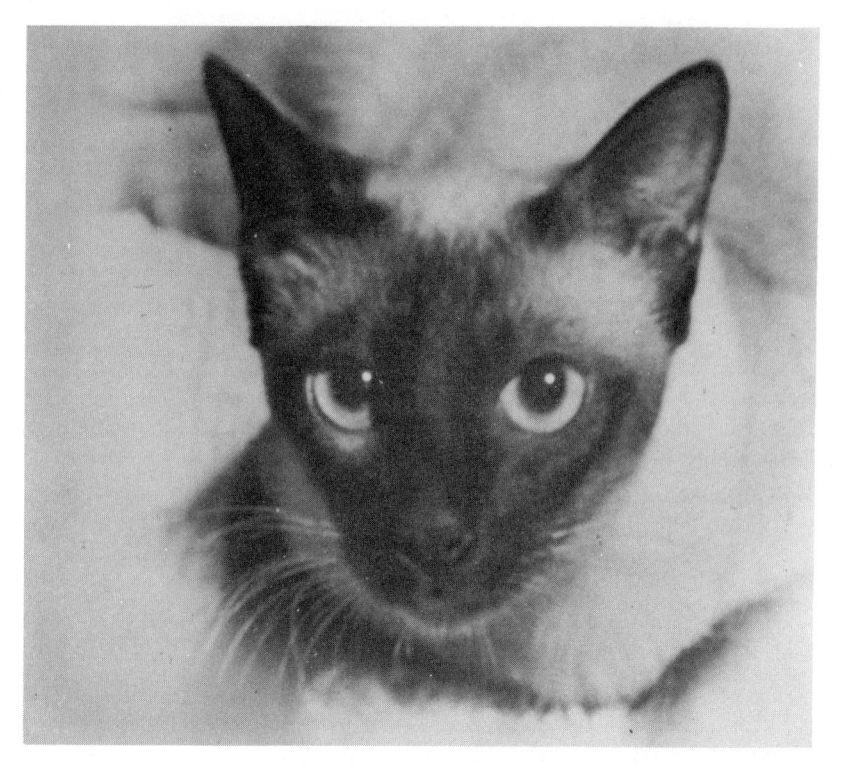

Seal Point female owned and bred by Mr. and Mrs. Clyde J. Murray: R.M. DBL. CH. MOON GLOW'S JINX. Sire: Judo's Bit-A-Frost of Moon Glow; dam: Fan-T-Cee's Miss T-C of Moon Glow.

Diarrhea

Simple digestive upsets evidenced by loose bowels and vomiting can be treated with remedies used for children. Kaopectate is good. This has an astringent action on the intestinal mucous membranes, which curtails the production of toxins and gas. Give the cat two to four teaspoonfuls, depending on the size of the cat, every two to four hours. This should relieve the diarrhea in a day's time. It is wise to eliminate all dairy products from the cat's diet for a few days, and feed solid foods only. If you suspect the upset is the result of a change in diet, go back to the original diet.

Non-specific, non-infectious inflammation of the digestive tract may be caused by various bacteria, heavy worm infestation, repeated de-worming, chills, foreign bodies, or impacted bowels. An infection could have settled in the digestive tract, or the symptoms may be a warning of a specific disease. If the condition remains for more than twenty-four hours, have your veterinarian diagnose the condition and prescribe an effective treatment.

Constipation

Hard or infrequent bowel movements suggest an adjustment is needed in the diet to produce a softer or more frequent stool. Try adding oil to the cat's food or offering him milk.

Poisons

Many chemicals are poisonous to cats. Particularly dangerous are DDT, Chlordane, and Lindane in any form, such as insecticide powder or spray.

Blue Point female owned by Mrs. Lydia E. Dzbanski, bred by Mrs. Fred Galvin: TR. GR. AND QUINT. CH. FAN-T-CEE'S WILL-O-WEE OF TAP-TOE. Sire: Kabar Will-O-The Wisp; dam: Zagazig's Chun Moi. Photo by "Muzzie."

Blue Point male owned and bred by Marge Naples: DBL. CH. DINAPOLI'S RHAPSODY IN BLUE II. Sire: Fan-T-Cee's Phoenix of Wolfgang; dam: DiNapoli's Blu-Willow. Photo by Hans Bomskow.

Many coal-tar derivatives, such as those containing carbolic acid or phenol compounds, are equally dangerous. Lead, such as that found in paint, can cause poisoning. Arsenic, usually found in weed or snail killers, can kill a cat. Read the label carefully to determine the contents of anything you use that your cat can possibly come in contact with. Be especially careful of lawn sprays, if your cat is allowed outside. It is not uncommon to see a cat eating grass. Even if he does not eat the newly sprayed grass, he could get some of the poison on his feet and then lick it off. Be very careful not to spray fly or odor-killing products where little kittens can inhale the fumes. They are very young and most susceptible, and this not only could cause them serious harm but could kill them.

If you suspect poisoning, proper emergency treatment is to induce vomiting with repeated doses of one tablespoonful of a mixture of equal parts of 3% hydrogen peroxide and water, until vomiting occurs. Try to identify the poison and, if possible, take the label and the cat to your veterinarian without delay. The label will indicate the antidote, saving valuable time in administering treatment.

Ringworm

Ringworm is a fungus, not a worm. It is the only common skin disease that can be transmitted from humans to cats and vice versa. This is no longer a serious problem—if you get prompt diagnosis, obtain proper medication,

Seal Point male bred and owned by Mrs. Madeleine Christy: DBL. CH. MADALI FASCINATION. Sire: Laurentide Thio (Imp) of Madali; dam: Na-Wi-Ta-Sooh Siwgh of Madali. Photo by John White.

Blue Point female owned and bred by Ruth M. Dingess: CH. RU PAU'S BLUET II. Sire: Ta-Lee-Ho's Al-la-Bi; dam: Shan of RuPau. Photo by Barr.

and faithfully administer it. New methods, using drugs such as griseofulvin that work from the inside when taken in pill form and from the outside when applied in cream form, have shown great promise for speedily eradicating ringworm, especially on short-haired cats. If your cat gets ringworm, in addition to treating the cat you should very thoroughly vacuum up all the loose hair around the house and scrub your linoleum floors, after isolating the cat.

Maggots

What a horribly unpleasant subject! I feel compelled to mention it, however, as I actually saw a lovely cat brought in to my veterinarian's office, where I happened to be helping out at the time, which had a great hole maggot-eaten in the muscle of each hind leg! Her owner had neglected her completely. It seems the cat had suffered a miscarriage and had crawled under a bush where she had lain in misery. When a cat feels extremely bad, it does not clean itself, and if allowed to remain with blood or fecal matter on the coat, the offensive substance soon attracts blow-flies or other flesh flies, which lay their eggs in such places. The eggs shortly hatch into maggots which immediately begin eating into the flesh. A flyblown wound crawling with maggots is not a very pretty sight.

The cat referred to did recover, and when her owner found she had a sizeable bill, she instructed the veterinarian to dispose of the cat, as she didn't care to pay the bill! Instead, the cat was placed in a good home where she receives tender, loving care, obviously a pleasant new experience for her. Please don't acquire a cat or any animal unless you think enough of it to take good care of it.

Eczema

Some cats are allergic to certain foods, and when they eat these foods their skin erupts into rashes or sores. Vitamin deficiency or *excess* can also result in skin conditions. Fleabites, compounded by the presence of fungus, are a common cause of skin trouble. Even certain flea sprays or powders may cause irritation.

After you have determined the cause, simply eliminate it, or give more vitamins if the cause is lack of them. If the skin reaction is severe, an anti-allergy shot can be given to relieve the symptoms. Baths with a medicated shampoo often will soothe and help clear up skin inflammation.

Seal Point female owned by Marjorie Buckner, bred by Harriet Wolfgang: R.M. CH. WOLFGANG'S SABRINA OF QUEEN CANADA. Sire: Killdown Monty of Wewan; dam: Wolfgang's Frau II.

Frost Point female owned and bred by Dr. and Mrs. Ralph Boren: R.M. DBL. GRAND AND QT. CH. BOREN'S LITTLE LADY LILAC. Sire: Frost-E-Lad of Boren; dam: Bograe's Lavender Lady of Boren.

Blue Point female owned by George Silva, bred by Gen Scudder: CH. ARISTA'S CHARMING OF SAI BAN. Sire: Arista's TiCiTu; dam: Arista's Blue Sprite.

Blue Point male owned by Mrs. Thomas Dugle, bred by Mrs. O. R. Schroeder: DBL. CH. KO-KO-MO- OF DEEARDON. Sire: Deeardon's Mombo; dam: Mieko Yoshamura. Photo by Robert Lodder.

Bites

A cat's skin heals very readily; thus, a deep bite wound will seal over quickly on top. Outwardly the skin may show no break, but infection may be building up in the wound and throughout the cat's system. Treatment consists of lancing and injections of antibiotic. After that, keep the scab removed and the wound cleaned out daily, as it must be kept open to heal from the inside out.

Bites from spiders and ants and other insects can produce a severe reaction in some cases. If a cat is bitten near an eye, the swelling can cause the haw to completely cover the eye. Other mysterious swellings may be due to insect-bite reaction, and usually subside in a day or so. They could require an allergy treatment.

Seal Point male owned and bred by Hazel and Hank Ludkey: R.M. QUAD. CH. RENDARA'S CHUCK-A-LUCK. Sire: Rendara's Luckey Buck; dam: Rendara's Falena. Photo by Victor Baldwin.

Teeth

A cat with a sore mouth will not want to chew or eat. Teeth should be checked for tartar accumulations. When tartar is present, the teeth should be scaled to prevent irritation of the gums and infection. Infected teeth should be removed. Infection from abscessed teeth or roots can spread throughout the cat's entire system.

Frost Point female owned by Clare Scott, bred by Mrs. Carey; QUAD. CH. KRIS-TEE FROSTINE OF GLORY-S. Sire: Glory-S Kris Kringle; dam: Fros-Tee Moon. Photo by Hans Bomskow.

Seal Point male owned by Leonille and John Smith, bred by Mrs. Tanya Hokin: R.M. TR. CH. DARK GAUNTLET'S VIBRATO. Sire: Dark Gauntlet's Sir Vivor; dam: Dark Gauntlet's Idol.

Cystitis

The urinary bladder is normally situated in the rear of the abdominal cavity, but when greatly distended it protrudes well into the abdomen. This is a symptom of cystitis. The bladder will feel hard and the size of an orange when the cat is unable to pass his urine. A cat with a full bladder acts anxious, uneasy, and listless, and has no appetitie. He tries unsuccessfully to urinate at frequent intervals, and will perhaps pass just a few drops. Often he will completely disregard his usual clean toilet habits. He may cry plaintively, growl or bite when touched or picked up, as the condition is extremely painful. Unless the urine is expelled and the bladder is relieved of this pressure as soon as possible, uremic poisoning develops, resulting in quick death. Just think of the cats running loose that suffer from this and die, their owners never even knowing what happened to them. It is a fairly common ailment.

One cause of stoppage is the formation in the bladder of material resembling fine grains of sand. These pack together and lodge in the small urethral passage, thereby plugging the outlet. The veterinarian will try to open this passage with a catheter and draw off the urine. He will then attempt to flush

Cats can be harmed by improper handling, as pressure exerted on sensitive areas can damage internal organs. This is the correct way to hold your cat, with adequate support given to two areas of the body.

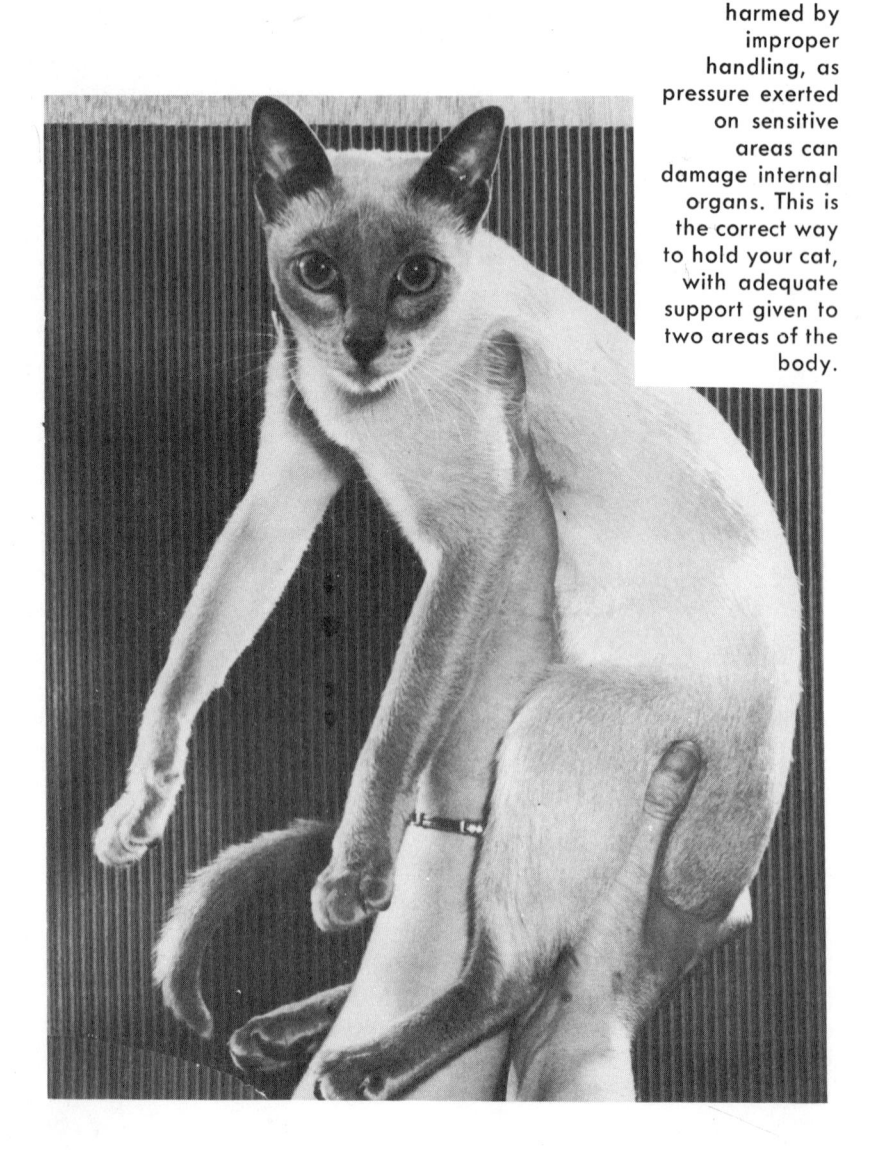

out the bladder and inject medicine. In more extreme situations, surgery is required. Sometimes it is necessary to continue expressing the urine manually and to repeat the catheterization because the bladder muscle becomes paralyzed due to the strain and can not function. Drugs are used to restore bladder tone and also to acidify the urine, helping to prevent future formation of sand. Special low ash diets are prescribed.

Another cause which produces the same result is a mucous, or puslike, plug. Blood is often present in the urine in this case; another symptom may be a high temperature. In a male cat, irritation may result from unsuccessful breeding attempts or too frequent breeding. If infection is present, antibiotics or sulfa drugs are given in addition to the other treatment described above.

In the female cat the passage, being larger, seldom closes entirely, and there is not the extreme emergency as with the male. However, females can get cystitis, which could entail serious debilitating effects. Occasionally, the female will also suffer from the inability to pass a sufficient amount of urine.

Anemia

Anemia, a deficiency in the normal amount of red blood corpuscles or of hemoglobin, or both, may be detected by looking at a cat's gums and tongue. If they are pale in color, it is possible that he is anemic and needs treatment. Have this condition checked by your veterinarian to determine the cause and treatment. Anemia may have simple or complex origins and must be treated accordingly. A liver and iron tonic with B complex vitamins added is valuable for the prevention of anemia in nursing mothers and young kittens, and to perk up a fussy appetite which may stem from slight anemia.

Aspirin

In an article appearing in the October 15, 1963 issue of the *Journal of the American Veterinary Medical Association*, authored by E. John Larson, D.V.M., it is stated that while for many years aspirin has been considered a safe, effective drug, it is not without toxic properties, and that recent investigations have shown that aspirin can be harmful and dangerous.

The experiments that Doctor Larson describes show that cats given one 5-grain dose of aspirin daily died after an average of twelve doses. Cats given one 2-grain dose per day survived, but both groups produced clinical signs (appearing after one or two doses and continuing for varying lengths of time) of depression, poor appetite, vomiting, loss of weight, drug intoxication, and pathologic changes in organs and tissues, and a toxic effect on bone marrow which had not been reported in man or other animals previously.

Lesson to be learned: Don't give cats or kittens repeated dosages of aspirin, a derivative of phenol known to be toxic to cats.

Blue Point male owned and bred by Mrs. Helen C. Koscak: GR. AND QUAD CH. KOSCAK'S LU-E-TU. Sire: Koscak's Luang II; dam: Koscak's Charmaine. Photo by Gordon Laughner.

Simple Cold

A simple cold may be treated with one or two very small doses of aspirin ($\frac{1}{2}$- or $1\frac{1}{4}$-grain children's size). If the cold persists or worsens, you should consult your veterinarian. A sore throat and runny eyes are often symptoms of something serious.

Convulsions

Convulsions are a symptom rather than a disease. They may result from a number of causes. Consult your veterinarian immediately for diagnosis and treatment.

Parasites

Generally poor condition, tacky coat, thinness even though the appetite is good, chronic loose bowels or bloody stool, an allergic skin reaction, each, or all, may be symptoms of parasitic infection.

Seal Point male owned by Mrs. Fredric Hokin, bred by Mrs. Fred Hoyt: CH. TYOH NUSTA OF DARK GAUNTLETS. Sire: Dbl. Ch. Cuthpa Nuzano; dam: Mao Seal Celesta of Tyoh. Photo by Hans Bomskow.

Blue Point male owned by Master John O. Naples, bred by Joli Smith: DBL. CH. JOLI'S MATADOR OF DINAPOLI. Sire: DiNapoli's Blue Tango; dam: Fan-T-Cee's Flamboyant.

Blue Point male owned and bred by Clare L. Scott. CH. GLORY-S KRIS-NITE. Sire: Glory-S Blue Danube; dam: Montecito Darpi-Dell of Glory-S. Photo by Hans Bomskow.

Tapeworms

This subject is also covered in the chapter on Grooming; as mentioned there, cats get tapeworms from fleas. The fleas eat the tapeworm eggs which are carried to the outside by the tapeworm segments passed out by the cat. The egg then hatches inside the flea and completes its larval development there. If the cat should swallow a flea with these larval tapeworms in it, he then will have tapeworms; therefore, both fleas and tapeworms should be eliminated. If fleas cannot be entirely eliminated they should be kept at a minimum so that the chance of tapeworm infestation is at least reduced. There are other types of cat tapeworms that have different intermediate hosts for their eggs, such as mice, gophers, and other small animals. Treatment for eliminating these types from the cat is the same, however.

The most evident sign of tapeworm is segments in the cat's stool that look like grains of rice. If you look carefully at one of these, you will see it moving. Consult your veterinarian. He will probably want to worm the cat for you, or he may give you the pills and instruct you how to do it. It is a messy job and your cat will be miserable during the treatment, but he will feel much better when it is over. The head of the tapeworm must be loosened and passed, or it will continue growing. In order to do this effectively, the pill must be sufficiently strong. It is usually given on an empty stomach. If the cat doesn't pass or vomit the worms within a couple of hours, he must be given an enema to rid his system of the poison contained in the powerful medications.

Roundworms

Evidence of roundworm infestation is found by fecal analysis made by a veterinarian. Also, these wiry, spaghetti-like worms often are vomited. Ascarids, or roundworms, do not require an intermediate host, unless you consider the cat himself the host. The larval stages of these worms develop within the cat. The adult roundworms lay eggs in the cat's intestines, and

Blue Point female owned and bred by Dorothy Braud: CH. DULCE DO-MUM'S MATSUH. Sire: Joli's Matador of DiNapoli; dam: Lady Thaing of Cassia. Photo by Hans Bomskow.

the eggs are passed out in his feces, thereby contaminating the ground. The host cat (and other cats) gets these eggs on his feet or fur, and when he washes, the eggs get back into his digestive tract. The roundworm larva hatches in the intestines and burrows into the intestinal wall. It then gets into the blood stream. If it migrates to the lungs, it completes its larval development in the air passages of the lungs, works its way up toward the mouth, is coughed up and swallowed. Upon reaching the intestines again, it becomes an adult worm and starts reproducing by laying eggs.

Not all larvae reach the lungs in their migration. Some wander aimlessly in the abdominal cavity for a while, and then become dormant, sometimes for

Chocolate Point female owned by Chuck Braud, bred by Helen Koscak: QUAD. CH. KOSCAK'S CHOCO DULCE. Sire: Koscak's Suko; dam: Koscak's Choco Vixen. Photo by Hans Bomskow.

Seal Point premier owned by Eva Lydick, bred by Mrs. S. L. Lydick: DBL. GR. AND QT. PREMIER HAI TAI BLACK MAGIC. Sire: Fan-T-Cee's Sir Cecil of Hai Tai; dam: Lamar's Cassia of Moontide.

many months. In female cats, pregnancy seems to activate these migratory larvae, the larvae migrating into the uterus and even into the embryonic kittens. They can complete their cycle within the kittens, actually causing the kittens to be born with roundworms. This explains why many litters of kittens are found to be infested when there is no known history of roundworms in the mother. Since fecal examination, the usual method of detecting the presence of roundworms, shows only that adult egg-laying worms are present in the intestines, if the roundworms are not in this particular stage of their cycle they cannot be diagnosed. If roundworms are present when a cat is given the medicine to eliminate tapeworms, the medication removes the roundworms, too. However, you can not give a small kitten the harsh medication necessary to eliminate tapeworm. To treat roundworms only, piperazine compounds, in recommended dosages, may be given directly or mixed with food. These are effective against the adult roundworms, but not against roundworm larvae or eggs, or tapeworm. Repeated treatment at weekly intervals is essential to rid a cat of roundworms. This medication does not make either a cat or a kitten ill.

Coccidiosis

This parasitic infection is caused by a protozoan organism which lives within the cells lining the small intestine. As these organisms complete their cycle and the eggs, or oocysts, are ready, the intestinal cell ruptures and permits their release. In the early stages of infection there may be a severe systemic reaction and fever. Diarrhea usually occurs intermittently. If the infection is not too massive and has been present long enough for the cat to build up some resistance, there may be no symptoms. Diagnosis is made only by fecal examination, which, along with treatment, is done by a veterinarian. Consistent bloody diarrhea may be caused by coccidiosis, particularly in young cats or kittens. Transmission to other cats is common and likely. It is usually passed on by the washing process, when feet or fur have become contaminated by contact with the feces of an infected cat.

Seal Point male owned and bred by Mrs. Fredric Hokin: QUAD. CH. DARK GAUNTLETS DAUPHIN. Sire: Tr. Ch. Dark Gauntlets Diminuendo; dam: Dark Gauntlets Delphinium. Photo by Hans Bomskow.

Frost Point female owned by Ruth M. Dingess, bred by Betty Corkhill: XANTIPPE OF RU PAU. Sire: Ta-Lee-Ho's Chocolate Chipper; dam: Chen Po Pei. Photo by Barr.

Ear Mites

As mentioned in the chapter on grooming, some cats have a rather dark waxy discharge in their ears, which is nothing to become alarmed about. However, if you see your cat dig at his ears and try to scratch at the base of them or lay his head over to one side and shake it, he may have picked up ear mites. Ear mites are extremely contagious—from one cat to another and to other animals, but not to humans. These mites themselves are tiny and white and are not visible to the naked eye. The irritation they cause in the ear canal produces a brown or black crumbly wax which is seen in and about the ears. The eggs must hatch before the contained larvae can be killed by medication, so if you think your cat has ear mites, see your veterinarian immediately. He will give the cat some initial treatments, and may give you a pesticidal oil to take home, showing you how to treat the ears yourself. Your cat won't appreciate your treatment, of course, because his ears are sore, but if you are consistent, the mites should be eliminated before long. If treatment is not administered promptly, there is danger of a secondary infection in the ears that will require treatment even after the mites are eliminated. If mites are not eliminated, they could drive a cat into a frenzy.

Ticks

Ticks are found nearly everywhere. In cattle-raising country, the spinose ear tick may get into a cat's ears when he goes where cattle graze. It is best that this type of tick be removed by a veterinarian.

Other species of ticks attach themselves to the cat's skin. In this case, they are usually found on the head and neck, where the cat can't reach them. If the head of the tick is not too deeply imbedded, remove it by gently pulling on the body of the tick. If it does not come off readily, sprinkle a little flea powder or place a drop of spray directly on the tick. In about a day, he will die and drop off.

Viral Diseases and Vaccinations

Rabies

Although any warm-blooded animal can contract rabies, cats are not usually vaccinated against it unless there is an "epidemic." However, this vaccination is required for certain interstate or foreign shipments.

Frost Point female owned by Clare Scott, bred by Mr. and Mrs. C. Perkins; GR. AND QT. CH. FELIS CLARUS REVERIE OF GLORY-S. Sire: Glory-S Kris Kringle; dam: Lady Mei Ling Frost. Photo by Hans Bomskow.

Blue Point male kitten owned by Helen Eastman, bred by Marge Naples: DiNAPOLI'S TANGO II. Sire: Fan-T-Cee's Phoenix of Wolfgang; dam: DiNapoli's Blu-Willow. Photo by Mark Eastman.

Blue Point female owned by Mrs. N. Leoni, bred by Mrs. E. Berger: TR. CH. JUDO'S BLUE SPARKLE OF SUNGLOW. Sire: Judo's Jack Frost; dam: Winsom Lass of Judo. Photo by Hans Bomskow.

Feline Enteritis

This is also referred to as feline distemper or cat fever. The proper name is infectious feline panleucopenia. Enteritis means inflammation of the intestinal tract, and is a general word used in diagnosis when there is intestinal infection. Cat fever is a swift killer.

When you are buying a kitten, be sure to determine whether or not he has been vaccinated for cat fever. If not, have it done immediately. The recommended age for vaccination of kittens is eight or nine weeks, or as soon thereafter as possible. A booster shot each year after the initial vaccination further protects a cat. Young cats are particularly susceptible to this killer disease, although a cat may contract it at any age. If you had a kitten or cat die of it, don't take a new kitten into your house until six months have passed, then give him all new bedding, litter box, toys—everything!

Onset of this disease is characterized by listlessness, extreme weakness, vomiting of a yellowish fluid, diarrhea of the same type fluid, and fever. The cat may hang his head over a water dish, craving to drink, but unable to do so. If you suspect cat fever, rush your cat to a veterinarian without a moment's

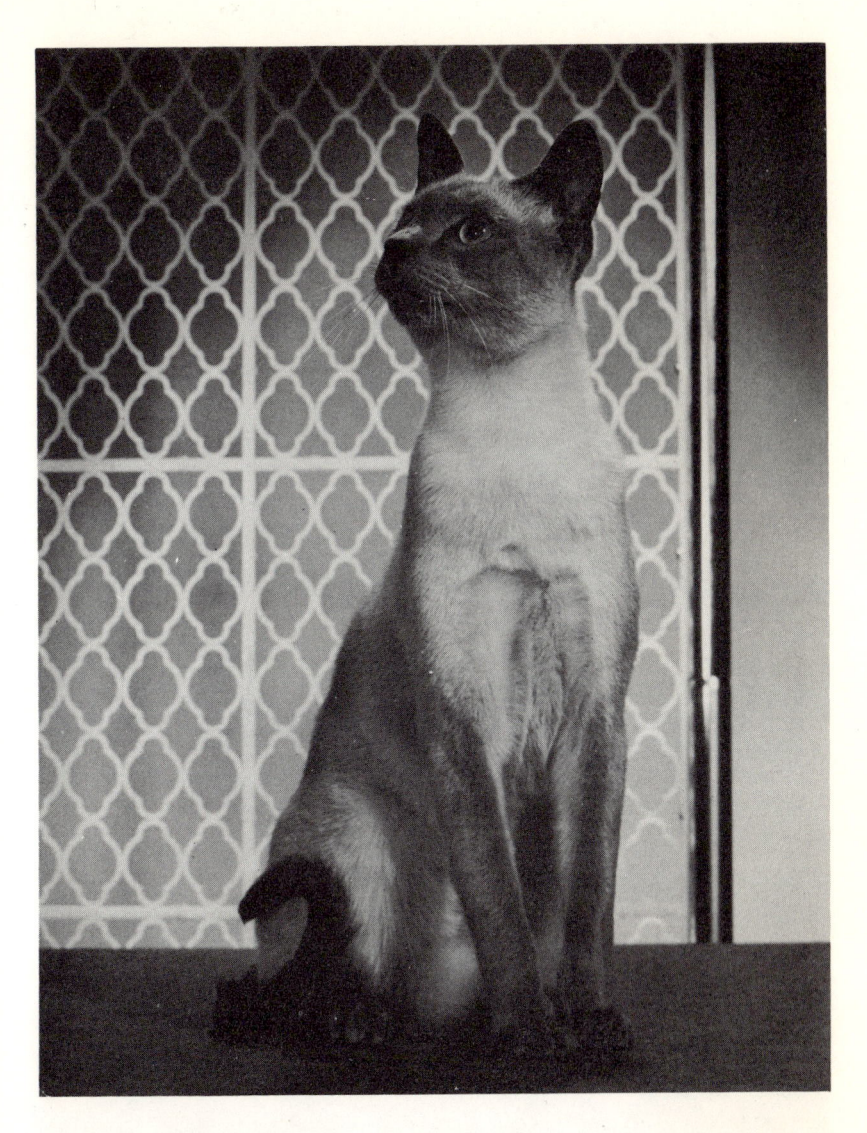

Blue Point male owned by Judy Magrum, bred by Mr. and Mrs. C. H. Krebs: R.M. TR. CH. KREB'S VALENTINO. Sire: Hi Tai's Saint Elmo's Fire; dam: Fan-T-Cee Fan Fayre of Kreb's. Photo by Victor Baldwin.

delay. The course of this disease is so swift it is sometimes mistaken for poisoning. The virus is passed by contact, either directly or indirectly, from areas contaminated by an infected cat. Dogs and humans don't get this disease, only cats. A vaccinated cat could become infected, but the chances of recovery are vastly greater than if he had not been inoculated against it.

It is possible for humans to carry cat fever to your cats and kittens on their shoes, if they have been where the disease existed. If you are selling kittens, be extremely careful about letting anyone handle them.

Pneumonitis and Other Respiratory Infections

Symptoms of these diseases in the feline resemble those of a severe cold in humans: the eyes water, the nose runs, the throat is sore, the sufferer coughs and sneezes, and seems to be sore all over. He is feverish, listless, and will not eat. Sometimes the bowels are loose. Treatment in the early stages gives the best and quickest results. When a cat shows any of the above symptoms, isolate him immediately, and isolate any cats he may have come in contact with, as all these respiratory diseases are spread through the air and by contact with articles that have been sneezed or coughed on.

Some respiratory infections are not as serious as pneumonitis, but since the early symptoms and treatment are identical, it is best to presume an

Frost Point female owned and bred by Clare Scott: TR. CH. GLORY-S KRIS-DELL. Sire: Glory-S Kris Kringle; dam: Gr. and Quad. Ch. Montecito Darpi-Dell of Glory-S. Photo by Victor Baldwin.

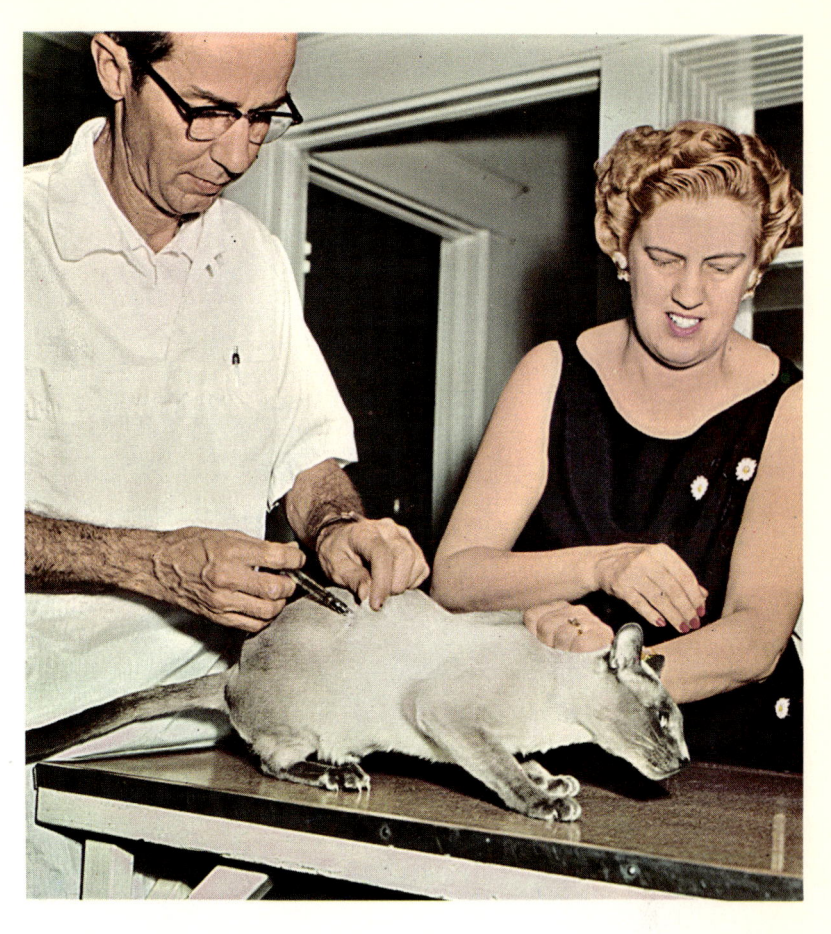

Dr. Phillip Ramsdale, D.V.M., inoculates a distinguished patient, DBL. GR. CH. SERENADE IN BLUE. Photo by Louise Van der Meid.

One of the prime attractions of the Siamese is that it provides the intelligent and sympathetic companionship so desirable in a true pet. Photo by Louise Van der Meid.

Alertly inquisitive, this Siamese mother (DINAPOLI'S RATANA KAN-YA) inspects her surroundings to make sure that there is no danger to her kittens. Photo by Louise Van der Meid.

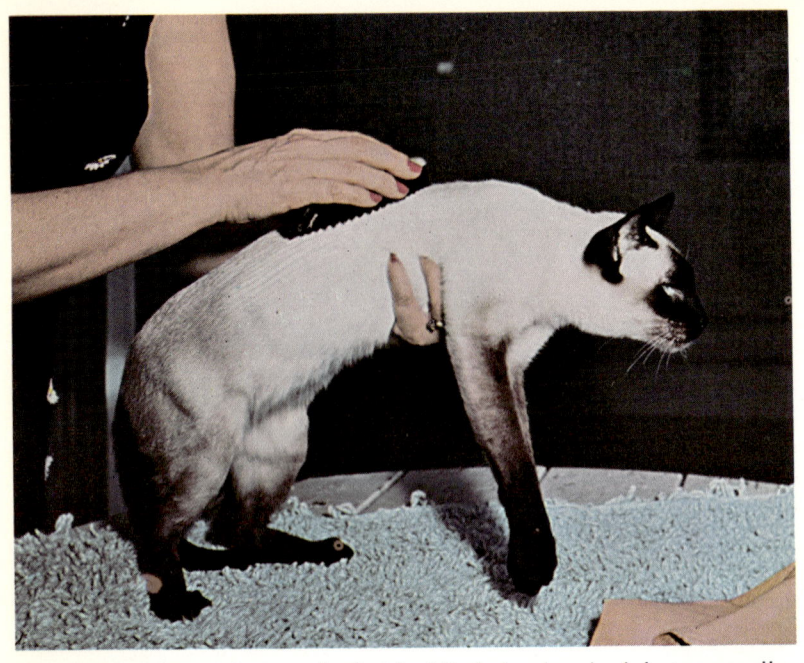

Sometimes Siamese have to be held while being brushed, but generally they enjoy their grooming period and the attention they receive during it. Photo by Louise Van der Meid.

Grandma PHET enjoys the solid contentment of curling up in her own comfortable basket. Photo by Louise Van der Meid.

Chocolate Point female owned by Harlan Hokin, bred by Mrs. Fredric Hokin: QUAD. CH. DARK GAUNTLETS VIGNETTE. Sire: Quad. Ch. Dark Gauntlets Sir Vivor; Gr. and Quint. Ch. Dark Gauntlets Idol. Photo by Hans Bomskow.

illness could be pneumonitis, and institute treatment accordingly. If it is merely a rhinitis, coryza, or similar coldlike condition, it will clear up fairly easily with treatment, and you and your cat are fortunate.

Pneumonitis is a killer, although its course is not as rapid as that of cat fever. The pneumonitis virus attacks the mucous membranes and causes the eyes, nose, throat, and intestines to become inflamed. It may go into the lungs, too. If the cat's throat is sore, it hurts to swallow. There is an extremely dangerous weakening effect in the cat's refusal to eat. Often force feeding must be resorted to. In extreme cases, feeding may be done successfully by a veterinarian with the use of an infant's nasal feeding tube.

The main problem is to find a food which will provide enough calories per volume and avoid diarrhea while sustaining the cat's life until the virus has been checked. One product that has been found satisfactory in both respects is Borden's Liquid Mullsoy. This condensed soy bean milk, if fortified with vitamins, seems to be able to sustain life and give the antibiotics a chance to do their work in controlling the secondary infections. Of course, you know that if antibiotics are given without food and liquid, they cannot produce the results they are expected to. Another very important factor in the treatment of pneumonitis is the maintaining of a continually warm, even temperature, with no drafts, together with a wealth of tender, loving care.

Blue Point female owned and bred by Marge Naples: R.M. SR. CH. DiNAPOLI'S BLUE CHIFFON. Sire: Fan-T-Cee's Phoenix of Wolfgang; dam: DiNapoli's Blue Willow. Photo by Hans Bomskow.

Blue Point male owned by Xenia Asta Agello, bred by Eloise and Frank Magnan. DBL. CH. ELO-YSE'S BLU-CHO OF SPICE CATS. Sire: Red Wing's Cho-Abi of Elo-Yse; dam: How Ling How Lovely of Royal Mask.

Several strains of pneumonitis viruses which cause similar symptoms have been isolated. Vaccinations have been developed against some of the more common ones, and they are a good precaution with which to fortify your pet. Immunity, however, is not long lasting, and vaccination has to be repeated periodically. It is possible for a recovered cat to have recurrences or be a carrier with few, or no, symptoms of chronic infection. He could infect other cats with which he comes in contact. The other kittens or cats could get the disease in severe form without any exposure being suspected. Particularly susceptible to the virus are kittens at weaning age, and cats and kittens whose resistance, for any reason, is lowered. Dogs and humans are not susceptible to these feline respiratory viruses. I have my veterinarian give my kittens their pneumonitis vaccination before the cat fever vaccination. Then they are building a resistance to these viruses as soon as they are weaned. If a strange cat who is a "carrier" of pneumonitis should wander in to visit, or if human visitors should bring the virus on their clothes, my kittens have some protection.

Hairballs

Siamese cats seldom get hairballs. It is possible, however. If you suspect that yours has a hairball, a small amount of Petromalt, obtainable at pet stores,

Frost Point male owned by Mrs. Edward Baker, bred by Clarence Perkins; QUAD. CH. FELIS CLARUS NARAI NICKI. Sire: Glory-S Kris Kringle; dam: Lady Mei-Ling Frost. Photo by Hans Bomskow.

usually will take care of it. Put some of this product on your finger tip and wipe it off on the roof of the cat's mouth. He will have to eat it to get it off. It does not have a bad taste, and cats seldom object to it. Some are rather pleased with its flavor. If you keep your cat brushed daily, he will never get hairballs, nor will there be excessive hair on your furniture or in your house anywhere. Brush him outdoors, preferably, so hair won't fly all over the room.

Gingivitis—Sore Gums

Certain bloodlines seem to be more susceptible to this problem than others. Gingivitis is seen as bright redness around the base of the teeth. Usually, it is caused by lack of vitamin C in the diet. Regular vitamin C pills for human consumption may be given to alleviate this condition. If left untreated, gingivitis could result in teeth falling out or having to be pulled out.

Stud Tail

Sometimes an unaltered male develops an oily substance on the top of his tail, near the base. When this condition is developing, it may be detected by the appearance of an oily, dirty patch under the fur on the tail. At this point, and before it goes any further, wash the tail thoroughly with a medicated soap and rinse until the hair "squeaks." Do this every day. If allowed to go on, severe blackheads develop, which may fester. This condition can progress to the point where the hair will fade and fall out, leaving the tail bare halfway down, or more. If blackheads have been allowed to develop, they must be removed before the condition will clear up entirely.

A similar development sometimes takes place under the cat's chin, requiring the same cleansing and blackhead removal.

CHAPTER X

CATTERIES

Evolution of a Cattery

It is an extremely rare occasion when anyone starts out from the beginning to have a cattery. Catteries evolve. For example, you love cats, and acquire a pet by one means or another. In looking around for the pet you see some very beautiful cats, but they cost more than you expect to pay, so you settle for something less. However, you never forget the lovely creatures you saw. You decide to have a litter of kittens, hoping they will resemble the cat you have in mind. So you try to find a stud cat that will sire exquisite kittens. You find his fee rather high and, again, you settle for something less. About sixty-five days later, your kittens arrive in healthy condition, and you love them

Chocolate Point male owned by Mrs. Lois Ross, bred by Mrs. Dorothy Braud: QUAD. CH. DULCE DOMUN'S EL COCO OF DINAPOLI. Sire: DiNapoli's Serenade in Blue; dam: Choco Dulce. Photo by Louise Van der Meid.

Blue Point female owned and bred by Mrs. Marjorie Elliott: DBL. CH. SHAN LING FAN-FARE. Sire: Fan-T-Cee's Fandango of Shan Ling; dam: Sky Hill's Ski-Lo of Shan Ling.

intensely. You keep one or two that you think are best, until you have an opportunity to show them. Don't feel too bad if your pet doesn't win Best Kitten in Show. It just does not happen by chance or with mediocre parents.

If you still want to produce a cat that will go to a show and win, keep the female you started with, and allow her to have kittens to help defray the expenses you now are running up. All cats eat, you know, and heartily, too. Search for and buy a good kitten to raise, and mate her to a fine stud. From this mating much nicer kittens will result. As your cat population increases, you will find it necessary to build a cage, then two, and still another, and more and more. After a while you discover that all this is very expensive and a lot of work. It can be heartbreaking, too, when sickness strikes and all your cats and kittens are fighting for their lives, with a great deal of help from you and your veterinarian, and even then you lose some.

However, if you love the cats and kittens, you will keep on trying, and eventually you will win a blue ribbon. By this time you are hooked, and your goal becomes a rosette, then a Best Cat in Show win, a Regional Award, and, possibly, a National Award. With each new success comes a higher goal, a bigger dent in your pocketbook, and a need for more cats, more kittens, and more cages.

The Ideal Cattery

Some suggestions for an ideal cattery follow:

A building insulated against both heat and cold, and one that is completely lined with some material that can be easily washed and sterilized.

In almost all climates, a heater with a thermostat and perhaps an air conditioner are necessary to maintain the cattery at continuously comfortable temperatures.

Cages that can be easily cleaned and easily partitioned into several smaller cages are best. All should be large enough for cats to walk around in, and should have shelves at different levels for the cats to jump up on and sleep. If you have the room, each cage should be large enough and high enough for a person to walk into.

These cages are arranged so that individual cats can be handled or removed without disturbing their companions. Photo by Louise Van der Meid.

A corner of Thani Cattery, owned by Mr. and Mrs. Noel Arthur. Notice the antiseptic cleanliness of the quarters and the presence of toys with which the cats may amuse themselves. Photo by Reed McCaskey, used with permission of the Meadville **Courier**.

The ideal cattery should be ventilated properly and should have an ultraviolet ray lamp to control contagious germs.

Each stud cat should have his own extra-large cage with a partition to separate him from the female until they get acquainted at mating time. If possible, the ideal is to have a separate, secluded stud room for mating.

Often females can live together in a very large cage. However, as each has kittens, she and the kits should have a cage to themselves.

Outside runs should be built in conjunction with the cattery so the cats can go out into the yard to run and play.

There should be a "work" area under which there are cabinets to house various supplies.

Seal Point female owned and bred by Gen Scudder: CH. ARISTA'S FAN FAN; Sire: Fan-T-Cee's LaLake of Rendara; Fan-T-Cee's Folie of Arista.

A Cage for One Cat?

With only one cat and a litter of kittens, it is convenient to have a cage to put the cat and kittens in, occasionally. When kittens get old enough to run around the house, they can be underfoot to the extent that you wish you had someplace to put them out of your way for a few hours. Further, if your cat should get sick, a place in which you can isolate him is a necessity. You don't want him sneezing and coughing all over everything in the house, or possibly "up-chucking" on your lovely new carpet or bedspread. Therefore, no matter how few cats you have, one or more cages are handy to have around. If you build them, make them big enough so a cat has room to move about, and use a material that will scrub easily. It is nice to have a shelf or two for them to get up on, and, of course, there should be a box for a bed, the litter box, and a dish of fresh water in all cages at all times.

A Novel Idea

One of our friends who is just starting a cattery has devised a wheel in one end of a large stud cage. The cat enjoys getting on the wheel and going for a good run whenever he feels so inclined. This is a wonderful way for a stud who must spend his life in a cage to obtain his exercise.

Cleanliness

All cages must always be kept clean. This means almost constant work. They should be sterilized thoroughly at least every single day to minimize the possibility of disease. Sound like drudgery? Believe it or not, I am much happier scrubbing my cats' cages than I am cleaning my house!

Actually, all the cats will be noisily complaining before I get to my cleaning chores, and before I have finished every cat and kitten is happy to be in a clean environment and each has had some individual attention. The kits and females have had a chance to romp, and by the time their romp is over and my work is done, they all settle down for a day-long nap, or at least to snooze until something or someone rouses them.

The Dispensary

After you have convinced your veterinarian that you are a breeder, he will sell you many of the simpler medications you may need and instruct you on their usage. After a while you will be able to spot trouble before it gets started. A dose or two of medication often nips serious complications in the bud.

Registration of Your Cattery

As pointed out in Chapter V, if you decide to register your operation as a cattery, choose a short cattery name and register it first with the Cat Fanciers Association, for the reason that practically every cattery is registered with this association. If you first clear with them the name you choose, you will be able to use the same name when registering with any of the other associations. You are required to send in three names. If the first name on your list is already in use, they consider the second choice; if that is in use, they take the third. The fee for registering your cattery with the Cat Fanciers Association is $10.00. This price is subject to change. Before you register your cattery with any association, contact the secretary or recorder of that association, who will be happy to send you a list of their fees, and a form to use in registering your cattery. The addresses of all the associations are listed in Chapter XIV.

Income Taxes

If your cattery is registered, and if you sell at least one kitten per year, you can set up your entire operation costwise on records from which you can report all your cattery expenses at the end of the year. However, you must report all of your cattery income. If there is a loss shown, it may be deducted from your regular income. If you show a profit (let me know, I'd like to see how it is done), it must be added to any other income and tax must be paid on it, accordingly.

I would suggest that for at least the first year you report your cattery operation, you consult a regular income tax accountant to advise you on exactly what is permissible as expense. All food, veterinary expense, registration fees, transportation expense to and from shows, transportation to and from the veterinarian, to and from airports to ship or pick up cats, expenses such as motel, meals, etc., while at a show, entry fees, subscriptions to any publications pertaining to your business, advertising, etc., all may be included in your cattery expenses. If you construct or buy a building to make into a cattery, the cost may be set up on a depreciation basis for income tax purposes. When you purchase a cat or kitten, his cost may also be depreciated over a number of years, but you may not depreciate the value of any kitten or cat that you have bred.

CHAPTER XI

STUD CATS AND QUEENS

Young Males

Sexual behavior in a male kitten usually becomes noticeable when he is between six and twelve months old. He will grab his sisters and brothers by the nape of the neck while they are all playing together, learning, as it were, by trial and error.

Spraying

Spraying is the act of wetting on drapes, furniture, and walls. This is a nasty development, but is it as much a part of the male cat as breathing is.

Blue Point female owned by Mrs. F. I. King, bred by Mrs. Frank Bjerring: GR. AND TR. CH. HOLLYWOOD ANGOVAR OF KING'S. Sire: Krampert's Ace; dam: Hollywood Krysette.

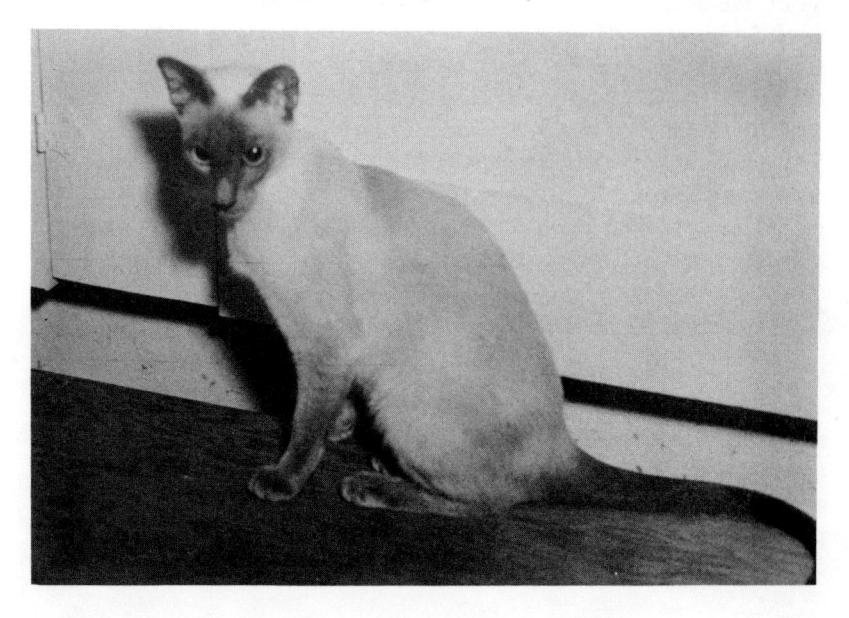

Some males will spray to a much greater extent than others. The decision between having him altered or putting him outside in a cage is not an easy one, but it is one that must be made. To put him out will break your heart (and his), at first, because he will not understand why is he suddenly being banished from sharing your life. Unless you intend to go into the business of breeding seriously, you and your pet will be much happier if you take him to your veterinarian for the minor surgery known as "neutering." This will not change his personality, but it will stop his spraying—if it is done before he is permitted to sire. He will not become fat and lazy, unless, of course, you feed him too much. He will make a much better pet after neutering, since his mind will not be preoccupied with sex.

If you decide to use him for breeding, a big cage such as that described in Chapter X is a prerequisite. You will find yourself spending a great deal of time outside with him. You will enjoy grooming and working with him and he will enjoy every attention you are able to give him. If you decide to take away his freedom, the very least you can do to compensate is to make him as happy as possible. Always keep his cage immaculate. He soon will become reconciled to the fact that this is his permanent home. He may protest loudly at first, but he will settle down, although it may take a few months.

Stud Cats

Stud cats are adult males used for breeding. Young males are generally not used for breeding until they are at least eighteen months old. In a few catteries, the adult males live together; in most catteries, each adult male is housed separately. Usually, a stud will become enraged at the smell of another male, and if these two are permitted to get at each other the results can be serious. They are not kidding, by any means, and if two males ever get into a fight they must be separated—but not with bare hands. Try to drop a blanket over one of them and pick him up quickly and pop him into a cage before he disentangles himself from the blanket. Another recommended procedure is to pour a large amount of water on both of them and then quickly get each into his separate cage.

To Locate a Stud

If your intentions are to breed your female cat, shop around well in advance of the time she will be ready to breed. Visit several catteries, meet the owners, notice the general conditions, and compare the studs and the catteries with others you have seen. If you know of no catteries, your veterinarian will probably know someone who has Siamese males at stud. Many times your pet store can help you find a stud. Try the yellow pages of your telephone directory. If there are no Siamese catteries listed, call any cattery. They

Siamese males love kittens and often do a good job of baby sitting. Here DINAPOLI'S SERENADE IN BLUE washes his kitten, DINAPOLI'S SHAMASH. Photo by Victor Baldwin.

usually are glad to put you in touch with the owner of a Siamese stud.

If there is a show in your area, attend it. Show catalogs contain cattery ads, as well as an alphabetical list of all exhibitors. Not only will you be able to locate owners of studs at a show, but you will enjoy seeing all of the cats. Perhaps you will see a male cat you particularly like. Find the owner and talk about the cat, his fee, and the background of your own cat. Notice which males win, and how many of the offspring of certain males win. Note the different characteristics of the cats.

Both *Cats Magazine* and *All-Pets* contain cattery ads that may help you.

Stud Fee

For a stud fee, you should expect to pay anywhere from $25.00 without papers to $100.00, which would include the male's pedigree. The bigger the title the stud cat has acquired through being shown, the higher his fee will be, and rightfully so. However, it is possible that the owner of the stud may want the blood line your cat represents and offer to take a kitten from the mating as part of the fee. If this is the case, be sure it is understood clearly whether the owner of the stud will take the choice kitten, the second choice, a male or a female, and what color. Always bear in mind that no breeder ever wants a kitten from an unregistered queen.

Another thing to be determined in advance of the breeding is whether or not you will be permitted to return your queen if the breeding doesn't take. Sometimes a young female won't conceive the first time she is mated and you will want to take her back for a repeat. Be sure you understand whether or not the fee discussed includes the papers on the male. The fee, of course,

Blue Point female owned by Phylis Sayer, bred by Mrs. Beaver: CH. BEAVER'S BLUE CHI ETTE de PHIL-BET. Photo by "Muzzie."

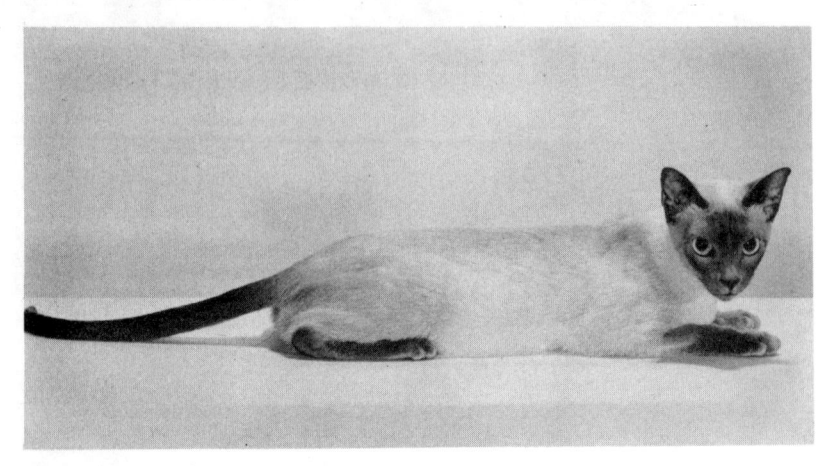

Blue Point male owned and bred by Mrs. Edwin Berger: JUDO'S HAPPY CHAP. Sire: Gr. and Quad. Ch. Judo's Jack Frost; dam: Win Sum Lass of Judo. Photo by Gordon Jarvis.

will be higher if papers are to be included. If you feel you won't want papers, the cost will be less, but in this case, ask how much the papers will be if you decide to obtain them at a later date.

Owners of studs know something about selective breeding, so listen to their advice. From the background of your female, they will be able to tell you which of their males will produce the best kittens with your female's bloodlines. The owner is very much interested in having the kittens sired by his stud do justice to him as breeder as well as to the quality of his stud. When the time comes for you to sell the kittens, it is possible that the stud owner may assist you to do so. He will be glad to help you pick out the best kitten, if you want to keep the best one and are in doubt as to just which kit it is.

Breeding is a specialized field. It should not be undertaken by a novice without careful consideration as to what is involved in time, effort, and adequate facilities for the care and sale of the prospective family. You are responsible for bringing these kittens into the world; you are definitely responsible for seeing that they are placed in good homes where they will receive the best of care. If you do want to have a litter of kittens, you will prevent costly errors by maintaining close contact with an experienced breeder and with your veterinarian through all phases of your venture. You will be repaid manyfold with a good healthy litter of kittens that will grow into lively intelligent loving little individuals. You haven't lived until you and your queen have raised a litter of kittens.

The Visiting Queen

Assuming that you have decided to mate your female and have found a proper male to breed her to, it is customary for the owner of the female to contact the owner of the male to determine a convenient time to send or take the female to see the male. It is entirely possible that the male may be working at stud that particular day, or perhaps be away at a show. It could even be that there is sickness in the cattery where the male lives and it would not be advisable for your cat to be there just then. It is also customary for the owner of the female cat to make sure the cat is in excellent health, has no worms, and has her claws clipped before going to be mated. She is quite apt to fight the male. He won't fight her, but she could catch him with a sharp claw and damage his coat, ear, eye or whatever. Quite often working studs are being shown, and of course their owners would not appreciate any harm being done

Seal Point male owned and bred by Mrs. Paul D. Ray: R.M. CH. SAMBO LAOHO. Sire: Cyreccia's Prince Oliver Wendall; dam: Cyreccia's Cheribonne.

Lynne Vanderpoel holds two of her show cats: (left) Blue Point female QUAD. GR. AND QUINT CH. VAN LYN'S PLATINE (sire: Sylvan Blu Pthalo of Vavar; dam: Criermere Li-She of Van Lyn) and (right) Frost Point male TR. GR. AND QUINT. CH. VAN LYN'S DILLY BOY (sire: Van Lyn Laddie; dam: Van Lyn Adilli).

to them. Studs are kept in peak condition at all times so that they will produce the best possible kittens. They are wormed periodically and their claws are kept clipped.

It is well to take, or send, the female to the male as soon as possible after real "calling" or "rolling" starts. The trip and arrival in strange surroundings will often put mating out of her mind. This is particularly true in the case of a pet cat. After a day or so of settling down, the urge will reassert itself and she will be agreeable to mating. The usual practice is for you to leave your queen at the cattery where the male lives for a couple of days. The owner of the male cat will probably call you when she is ready to be taken home. He will have witnessed several matings so he will be able to assure you that your queen has been mated. If you have decided on a stud cat that lives far away and you ship your cat to him, his owner will be happy to meet the plane, assuming you notify him of the arrival time.

When making your arrangements, you should determine how long the

Blue Point female owned by Vivian Wheaton, bred by Marge Naples: CH. DiNAPOLI'S TANG-A-BI BLU OF MALOJA. Sire: DiNapoli's Blue Tango. dam: Miss Al-La-Bi of DiNapoli. Photo by Eric Wheaton.

female will stay. Some catteries return females immediately after they have been mated. Others keep the female until they are sure the breeding has taken, thus saving you the cost of an extra trip back to the stud's home. This is especially true if the queen being shipped is being mated for the first time, because quite often the young queen's first mating won't "take."

Heat, Season, or Calling

Many a new owner is anxious for his kitten to grow up so she may have kittens. These eager individuals watch a young cat's every move, and when they think she is doing something unusual, they are absolutely positive she is in "season." They lose no time in calling to arrange a mating. It is not good to breed a female before she is a year old. It is also not advisable to breed her the first time she does "call." It is very annoying for the owner of a stud to have a female in that is not in "heat." The breeding won't take, and the cat must be returned to the stud at a later date. After your cat has come into season a few times, there can be no doubt in your mind that she is in heat. She will call so loudly it will sound as if she is screaming. She will roll on the floor; she will crouch on the floor and "pad" with her hind feet; she will lay her tail over to one side while padding; she will be extremely loving, even to being amorous with a chair or table leg. If you pick her up, she will stiffen out in your arms.

The time lapse between one season and another is variable. Some cats come into heat only a few times each year; others are out of season only a few days before calling again. Female cats will continue to come into season according to their individual time schedule, until they are bred. A cat that has just had kittens and is still nursing them can, and often does, come into season, and she can become pregnant immediately, if allowed to do so. If this happens, it is very hard on her. Most breeders try to see that their queens have only one litter of kittens each year, but there are instances when a cat will be almost continually in heat if not bred. If this is the case, it is best for the queen to be bred before a year has elapsed. Being constantly in heat may be a result of cystic ovaries.

Cats Differ From Other Animals

The ova, or eggs, of a female cat are not present waiting to be fertilized by the male sperm, as is the case in many other animals. The ovulation is induced by the sexual act itself. The size of the litter is dependent primarily on the number of eggs the female produces to be fertilized at that specific time; the male has no appreciable influence on the size of the litter.

Seal Point female owned by Mrs. Elizabeth Warfel, bred by Mrs. A. H. Watts of England: QUAD. CH. DU-BU FAITH OF DOMINEAU (IMP.) Sire: Beau Bosun; dam: Beau Belle.

Double Mating

Rarely, a cat that has been bred by one male will get out and be bred by another. It is entirely possible that she will conceive from each mating. Therefore, it is very unwise to permit your female cat to run loose after she has been mated to the desired male, until you are quite sure she has finished her cycle of heat, which may not be until several days after mating. The fact that a female cat has been bred does not automatically mean that she will immediately stop calling or go out of heat.

Unplanned Matings

A commonly mistaken notion is that if a cat mates with another variety of cat she is ruined for future breeding. This is ridiculous. One family of kittens, by whatever type father, has no bearing whatsoever on any future families.

They Do Have to Learn

It is usually best to mate an experienced stud with a young female being bred for the first time, and an experienced queen to a young male for his first try at mating.

CHAPTER XII

MOTHERHOOD AND KITTENS

(ARRIVAL OF KITTENS—CARE OF MOTHER AND KITS)

When to Expect The Kittens

The owner of the cattery where your queen was bred will tell you the day on which you should start the count. Sixty-three to sixty-six days after a cat is bred, her kittens will arrive. All of our queens deliver on the sixty-fifth day. If the sixty-seventh day goes by and nothing happens, it is wise to

Seal Point female CH. SIAMALKIN SHIBUI OF DEMBI'S, owned and bred by Esther E. Illingworth, proudly inspects her five-weeks-old Seal Point kitten.

197

consult your veterinarian. In the last days before the kittens are born they grow very rapidly, and if they are not delivered, you can see trouble is ahead. Actually, each week of a cat's pregnancy may be considered as corresponding to a month of human pregnancy.

Symptoms of Pregnancy

There are no outward physical signs of pregnancy in the female cat until about four weeks after breeding. The first sign, or change, noticeable is in her nipples. They will become a very much brighter pink and begin to enlarge. About this same time, you can feel a fullness in the lower rib area. Of course, from this time on, your queen becomes increasingly larger, and in a few more weeks, you can see and feel the kittens moving.

Some pregnant females vomit their food for a few days about two weeks after having been bred. This is morning sickness.

Feeding the Mother Cat

After your queen is bred, feed her as usual, and add a bit more calcium and vitamin D to her diet. Calcium can not be adequately assimilated without vitamin D. Be sure she has her regular vitamins. She needs to keep her strength up to produce plenty of milk for the little ones. Maintain the increased supply of calcium and vitamin D while the kittens are nursing, as this is a drain on the mother's calcium. Increase her feedings in both volume and number after the kittens are born.

Eclampsia

Eclampsia is the result of excessive calcium depletion from the system of a nursing or pregnant cat. The giving of any calcium product with vitamin D added is advised as a preventive. If you have not given your queen sufficient calcium and one day find her hiding in a dark corner, obviously sick and possibly drooling, rush her to your veterinarian. If you happen not to find her in sufficient time, she could be dead in a matter of a few hours. If you get her to a veterinarian in time, she may be saved with no undesirable after effects. If this happens and she is nursing, do not let the kittens continue to nurse. Dry her milk up and take good care of her. You will have to hand feed the kits if they are not old enough to eat on their own.

Miscarriage

It is possible for miscarriage to occur at any time during the nine weeks carrying period, and, sometimes, without your knowledge. The embryos may either be passed out or resorbed. At four to five weeks, the size of the

Blue Point female owned by Master John O. Naples, bred by Joan Poland: DBL. CH. MISS AL-LA-BI OF DINAPOLI. Sire: Ta-Lee-Ho's Al-La-Bi; dam: DiNapoli's Pu Nane. Photo by Victor Baldwin.

fetus and its placenta, not counting the water sac, is approximately half the size of the human thumb. This is the time the death of the fetus is most likely to occur. If it is passed out, the solid part may be unnoticed in the litter box or may be done away with by the mother cat. If the fetuses and other material in the womb liquefy, they are resorbed into the mother's system. Causes of death of kittens in the fetal stages vary: the egg or embryo may have been weak to start with or the fetus may not be developing properly; the mother cat may have a slight uterine infection which could kill the kittens but not affect her condition enough for you to be aware of it; some queens seem unable to carry kittens beyond a certain time; and sometimes the particular sire to which a queen is mated has lethal factors that kill the fetuses. If the last mentioned is the case, the queen may be mated to another male; the kittens will survive. Shock, injury, or excessive jumping in the later stages of pregnancy could cause a miscarriage or premature delivery. It is wise to keep the expectant female caged the last two weeks before delivery. She does not realize she is heavy and out of proportion and she will try to jump as usual. A miss and a nasty fall could result in a miscarriage or broken legs for the kittens.

As Delivery Nears

The pregnant female will start looking for a "nest" a few weeks before the kits are due. She will search out dark closets, shelves, and drawers and will dig and arrange and rearrange rags, papers, or clothes. Owners usually fix a nice big box with clean towels or blankets for their expectant queen, but she prefers to find and make her own nest. You will finally have to insist that she use the box you have prepared for her, or she will invariably end up delivering the kittens in your bed while you are sleeping in it. If she is caged, or course, this could not occur.

The Day of Birth Arrives

A day or so before the kits are due, your queen will start to follow you everywhere you go whenever she is out of her cage. She does not want to be alone. She wants the reassurance of your presence. If the litter is her first, she won't quite know what to expect, but she knows something is going to happen soon. Cats can have their kittens alone, but our cats are used to having all their needs taken care of. They are attached to us and want our companionship at this time, especially. Quite often your queen will wait for you to come home, or wake up or finish your work so you can give her your undivided attention before she will have her kittens. On one occasion, we got up in the morning and went to see how our expectant queen was doing. She was waiting for us — within twenty minutes, we had four lovely little kits! Many

Blue Point female owned by Natalie Leoni, bred by Mrs. E. Berger: TR. CH. JUDO'S BLUE SPARKLE OF SUNGLOW. Sire: Judo's Jack Frost; dam: Winsom Lass of Judo. Photo by Hans Bomskow.

times I have finished up my work late in the evening and been so tired I could hardly keep my eyes open, only to realize an expectant queen was getting ready to deliver. So we'd be up two or three more hours or longer.

I have found it is much easier to take into the kitchen the box previously prepared for the queen, or even clean out a drawer in the kitchen for her to deliver in. If you leave your queen for a minute, she will follow you. In the kitchen you are close enough to reach a pair of scissors that you have simmering in water, or you can attend to usual duties, if the waiting is long. If you are in the room and nearby, she usually will not get out of her box or drawer. You will know the kittens are on their way into the world when you notice a mucous discharge from the queen. Soon her "water" will break, and pronounced labor will begin shortly thereafter. Siamese kittens are smaller than those of other cats and, as a rule, the mother cat does not have a hard time delivering them.

The Uterus

A cat's uterus has two sides, or "horns." It is shaped like a short-stemmed letter "Y." Kittens are usually carried in both horns. At the time of birth, the kits are packed in tightly like peas in two pods. Each kitten born has a 50-50 chance of being presented for delivery in a breech position. (That is, hindquarters first.) If the head is first, the birth is easier, as the shape of the head is more suited to forcing its passage through the pelvis. There is no way to turn a kitten end-for-end inside the mother after the uterus has contracted around it during labor.

Breech Birth

If a kitten is coming "breech," grasp as much of the kit's body as you can with a piece of towel (so he won't slip out of your fingers) and pull gently down when the mother bears down. Let the queen rest a minute; when she bears down again, gently pull as she pushes. DON'T PANIC. If you pull too hard or pull too steadily, it is possible to rupture the queen's uterus. Work with her calmly, *gently*, and firmly. (A breech birth is not always difficult for the mother; don't attempt to help the queen unless she needs help.)

The Sac and Placenta (Afterbirth)

Each kitten is completely encased in a sac, or membrane bag, that is filled with liquid. The kitten "swims" around inside his sac. He gets his oxygen and food supply before birth from the mother cat. The placenta, or afterbirth, is attached to the mother's uterus. The kitten in the sac is connected to the placenta by the navel cord. This cord is about two inches long and is the pipeline from the placenta. At birth, the uterus begins to contract and pushes the kitten downward for his entrance into the world. The placenta detaches from its place on the uterus wall at that time and the kitten is on his own.

Removing the Sac

There is enough oxygen left in the blood of the placenta to supply the kitten for a reasonable time. However, if birth is delayed too long, the kitten will suffocate. When the kitten is clear of the birth canal, wait a minute to see if the mother cat will break the sac with her tongue. If she does not do this quickly, do it for her with a piece of towel. "Cutting the cord" may wait in favor of getting the kitten's nose clear of the sac so that he can begin to breathe.

Severing the Cord

The mother cat severs the cord by eating the sac and cord to the proper length. She stops chewing about a quarter-inch from the kitten's body. When we were learning this phase of the business, we needlessly lost a kitten because the mother cat cut the cord too close. Ever since then, we have done the job for our queens, and all of them have come to depend on us to do it.

After the kit is breathing and the mother cat has cleaned him for a minute, we find the cord. About an inch from the kit's body, we pinch the cord and roll it to curtail the blood. We take dull scissors which have been simmering in water and cut the cord in front of our fingers, away from the kitten's body, and roll the end attached to the kit between thumb and forefinger until the bleeding stops. Cutting with dull scissors has the effect of the mother's teeth in crushing the cord, which helps to stop the bleeding by sealing the blood vessels in the cord. The cord may be trimmed to a shorter length with sharp scissors, after it has dried.

Removing Fluid From Lungs

If a kitten doesn't seem to be breathing, we quickly cut the cord and pick him up to see if we can help him to breathe better. If there is mucus in his lungs, you can hear it and feel it. Place the kit in the palm of your hand, with your forefinger supporting the little head from behind, and shake the kit with a downward motion similar to that of shaking down mercury in a thermometer, being sure to support the head so you don't snap it. This will make the kit gasp, and gravity will pull the fluid and mucus out of his lungs. Wipe the mucus off as it appears. Repeat the shaking and wiping process until his breathing is quiet. Hold the kit close to your ear and listen for rasping or rattling noises, which mean there is some fluid present.

If the kit is having a bad time getting started with his breathing, rub him briskly with toweling, or you may try to force air into his tiny lungs by breathing into his mouth. A quick immersion of his body into cold water may shock him into taking a big gasp which may be just enough to get breathing started. Warm him up immediately, of course, by brisk rubbing with a towel.

Stimulating Circulation

Mother cats wash and tumble kittens about vigorously as soon as they are born. This hard washing makes the kitten cry and get air into his lungs. It also stimulates circulation and dries the wet fur. If you notice a kit turning blue, take him up and rub him briskly with a piece of towel. Shake him as described above to make him gasp and get air into his lungs. When you have checked him over and he is breathing well, give him back to his mother, as she will be worried about what you are doing to him. She will clean him up, and he probably will start nursing. As more kits arrive, perhaps you can take them away one at a time and put them in a dry warm nest, such as a wool sock, to sleep until their mother is finished with delivering kittens. The kits usually are tired by this time and will sleep. After all, they have just finished the most difficult journey of their life. Don't take a kit away from the mother until she is busy with another, or she will become very upset (if she hears kits crying, she will start to hunt for them). Everything will go along better without several little guys in the way.

Nine-months-old DBL. CH. MEDICINE LAKE WEE-SAL, bred and owned by Mrs. Adolph Olson. Sire: Chirn Sa-Hai Weasel of Carousel; dam: Medicine Lake Coquette.

The Placenta (Afterbirth)

The mother cat will eat the placentas. Don't be horrified. In the jungle, a mother cat was unable to hunt for food and get water for herself for a few days after giving birth, and eating the placentas may have provided nourishment to carry her through those days. The placenta has various hormone substances that her system needs, and it acts as a physic to clear out wastes. However, it is not necessary for the tame cat to eat all of the placentas. After she has devoured two or three of them, the remainder may be disposed of. Each kitten has an individual placenta, unless they happen to be twins or triplets. Be sure an afterbirth follows the last kitten born. If allowed to remain in the uterus, it could cause serious infection.

Are There More?

It is very difficult to tell whether or not there are more kittens to come. Sometimes a queen will have only one kitten. The usual litter for Siamese is four or five. However, there are those that have from nine to fourteen!

Fix a Clean, Dry Nest

As you know, it is uncomfortable to sleep in a damp bed, so remove all the wet materials, and fix a nice clean bed for the new little family. Place the kits in this clean box and the mother cat will jump in with them and resume her purring, which will have seldom stopped throughout the delivery. Quite often at this point she will have another kitten! If not, put the box away in a quiet closet and let the new mother and family sleep. The mother is worn out by this time. Put some fresh water down for her, as she may be thirsty. She will come out to see you when she has rested, and she will be hungry.

Get Acquainted With Your New Family

After the new little family has rested, you are naturally anxious to see if each of the kittens is all right, how many of each sex there are, and everything about them.

You probably already know all Siamese kittens are born pure white, with the exception of their pink bellies, which are pink because they have no hair on them as yet. The little whiskers and claws are already formed, and their eyes are closed, of course, and remain so until five days or so of age, when they begin opening. This is much earlier than other kinds of kittens open their eyes. Their little ears, too, are closed tight at first and open up as they develop. After a day or two, you will see a kit's nose begin to get a little color, and the edges of his ears and his tail will start to color, too.

Unless you know your stock well from past experience, or you know from your breeding that they will be all one color, you won't be able to tell what color the kits will be for about two weeks. If your mother cat is a Seal Point and you mated her to a Seal Point, and if both these cats are carrying Blue Point genes in their backgrounds, you will have Seal Points in the litter, but you may also have Blue Points. Do not be alarmed at this. A kitten is either a Blue Point or a Seal Point: he is not a cross between the two. Some of these kittens will carry only Seal Point genes, some will carry both Seal Point and Blue Point genes, and the Blue Point kittens will carry only the Blue Point genes. You will not know what the individual Seal Point kittens are carrying until they reach adulthood and reproduce. Unless you are establishing a cattery and going into the business of raising and showing cats, this will not be important to you. You will be very happy with your kittens; if there is more than one color in the litter, you probably will be delighted. It is fun to watch kits just hours old fight for a nipple! One day when you are looking at your new family and everything is quiet, you will hear a very tiny little "put, put," and it will be a baby purring already.

It is well to check each kit every day to be sure his tummy is full. Sometimes, in big litters, one won't be quite as strong as others, and they will push him away from the teats until he is too weak to fight his way through the mob.

Delivery on Two Different Days

I have known of female cats to have one or more kittens one day, and then another one, or more, as long as 48 hours after the first kit arrived. This is possibly the natural result of different conception times; often if more than twelve hours elapse between the first and last kitten's arrival, the later ones will be dead. Sometimes these dead kits are delivered normally, at other times surgical help is needed.

Premature Kittens

Some females do not carry to full term. Kittens born prematurely by more than one or two days generally have a poor chance of survival. They look and are small and naked when born, as compared to a full-term kitten. They do not have enough hair on them or enough fat under their skin to keep body heat in or protect them from chilling in the air. The hair and the little bit of fat are the things that fill out in the last week of pregnancy. The premature kitten's organs are not quite ready to work on their own. The kittens usually are too weak to nurse.

Care of Premature, Weak, or Orphan Kittens

The main need of newborn kittens is to be thoroughly dried and kept warm. Put them in an old wool sock, sweater sleeve, glove, or mitten. The wool is porous enough for them to get air. They then may be kept in a small, deep box, basket, or drawer. A purse sometimes fits the bill. A heating pad on very low or a hot water bottle may be put in with the kittens to keep them warm, or they may be placed over the pilot light of a gas range, in a box with an extra-heavy bottom. Be careful not to get them too warm.

Very little milk is required at first. A few drops of a mixture of half evaporated milk and half warm water is enough at a time. This should be given every hour or two around the clock until the mother is strong enough to take over. Do not try to feed a new-born kitten that is too weak to swallow or you will drown it. The kitten will continue to gain strength without feeding for a period of several hours, if kept warm. This strength comes from glycogen which was stored in his liver before birth. Many kits have been lost due to

His meal completed, one kitten leaves his nursing littermates and sets off on one of the adventures of his young life. Photo by Louise Van der Meid.

This mother Siamese will wait until her kittens are finished before she begins her own meal, and the interim provides a convenient opportunity for some extra diligent cleaning. Photo by Louise Van der Meid.

A young Seal Point male, TR. CH. DINAPOLI'S FASCINATION. Sire: DiNapoli's Serenade in Blue; dam: DiNapoli's Ratana Kanya. Owned and bred by Marge Naples. Photo by Louise Van der Meid.

over-anxious feeding attempted before their swallowing mechanism was strong enough to work. A tiny kitten is unable to pass urine or have his bowels move without help. Gently massage the genital area and stomach with a piece of damp cotton each time you feed him. Keep stroking until elimination stops.

The easiest way to care for orphan kittens is to find another cat with kittens the same age. Most cats will take strange kittens, which means the foster mother does not have to be a Siamese. Any mother cat will do. As implied, a Siamese mother will care for any other kind of kitten. Place the new kitten for the mother to "find." Her maternal instinct is aroused by the helpless baby's or babies' crying, and she will usually take them to care for without question, especially if you have rubbed the smell of her own kittens onto the new ones. If you plan to offer her the kittens, offer them bottom first. No mother cat can ignore a bottom to clean! Sometimes a bit of butter rubbed on the kitten's head gets the foster mother to lick the baby. Once she cleans the little one, she will accept it.

If for any reason you anticipate trouble with your kittening queen, it would be wise to breed another female at the same time so that the kittens of both would arrive at approximately the same time. If one queen should have trouble, the other could take care of all the kittens until the queen in trouble could get back on her feet, at which time she would pitch in and either take over her own kits or help with the entire group.

Abnormalities

Please remember that all of the following conditions are the exception rather than the rule. Most Siamese queens have no trouble whatsoever having kittens; most kittens are fine and healthy. However, the following things do happen occasionally:

Intestines Outside the Body

Occasionally kittens arrive with their intestines outside the body. This is due to the fact that the sides of the stomach wall do not knit together in the middle as they should before birth. It is a miscue in the embryonic development. Nothing can be done to remedy this situation, unless the unclosed gap is very small and the intestines can immediately be put back uncontaminated, and confined by a stitch or two. Kittens with this condition are born alive and may remain alive for some time, contrary to expectation.

Cleft Palate

A malformation that cannot be remedied is a cleft palate, a condition where the roof of the mouth is not closed and opens directly into the nose. Kittens suffering this malformation cannot nurse and will not survive. There is nothing to do but to destroy the kitten. It is well to check each kit's mouth by opening it and looking into it. If you don't check each kitten as it is born, the condition soon may be detected because milk will come out his nostrils. This is usually an inherited defect rather than one due to improper development of the cells in the embryo. It would be unwise to repeat the breeding.

Open Eyes

Occasionally a kitten will be born with his eyes open. The eyes of a newborn kitten are not ready to be exposed to the air, and such kittens may become blind. Many times such a condition is due to the fact that part of the firm edge of the upper or lower eyelid is not formed properly, failing to permit the eyelids to come together properly to protect the eye. Sometimes the eye itself is not affected, if light is kept from it, but trouble with hairs from above or below the eyelid poking into the eye will ensue as time goes on; it is possible to correct this with surgery. This problem may result from lack of proper vitamin intake by the mother cat while she is carrying her kittens. It could also be an inherited defect and, as such, should not be perpetuated. I have seen only one kitten with this condition. Its appearance was peculiar. I concur with another author who recommends that a kitten with his eyes open at birth should be destroyed.

Flattened Rib Cage

This condition is not uncommon. I understand a kitten can live with this deformity and be otherwise healthy. However, he would not have normal lung capacity and would require special care all his life. I believe it would be a kindness to put him to sleep. This condition might go unnoticed for some time after a kitten is born. We had one that began to develop this condition. He was half the size of his littermates, and I watched him closely. While trying to gather enough courage to take him in to my veterinarian to have him destroyed, I held the kitten quite often for extended periods of time, and as I did I held his little rib cage in the shape I wished it would develop (the first few days of a kitten's life the bones are very soft and pliable). I was also careful to see that the other kittens didn't sleep on top of this tiny one and that he had plenty to eat. After several days had passed, I was delighted to note that his rib cage was developing properly. I am happy to report that this kitten is today healthy and happy. I did, however, see that he went to a home where he would be altered, as I feel he lacked good breeding potential. This one experience in correcting a flattened rib cage is hardly conclusive, but it appears to have worked this time.

Euthanasia (Painless Destruction)

If you have to destroy a kitten, the best and easiest way is to take it to your veterinarian, who will put it to sleep painlessly. If you cannot reach your veterinarian, dispatch the kitten in the most humane way open to you.

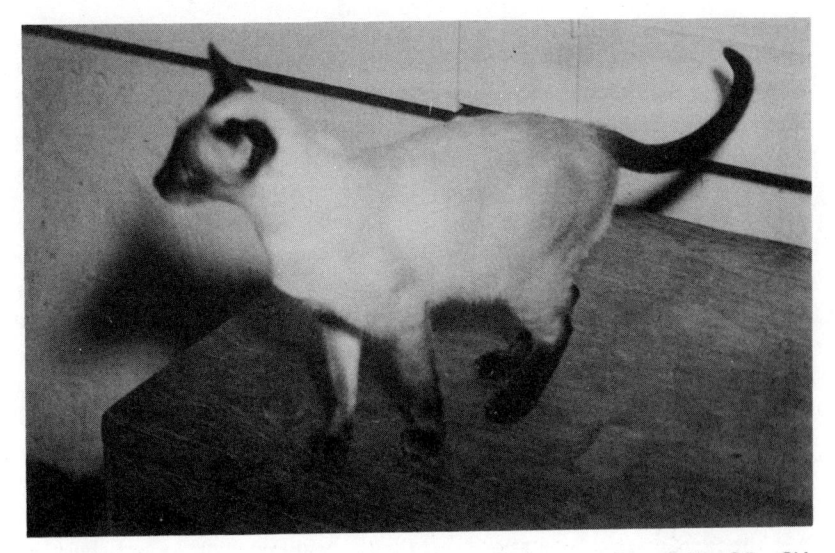

Seal Point female owned and bred by Mrs. F. I. King: R.M. GR. CH. KING'S KARESS. Sire: Medicine Lake KoKo of Phil-Lori; dam: Capri's Can-Dee.

If Your Queen Is in Trouble

This does happen, but it is the exception rather than the rule. When a female has been in hard labor (contractions that make her whiskers pull together) for two hours or more and no kittens have arrived, take her to your veterinarian. She probably needs his help for delivery. If you have any doubts or uncertainties about the wellbeing of your female at *any* stage of her labor, consult your veterinarian immediately. The uteri of some females do not have the required "tone," or push power, to expel the kittens. Injections of posterior pituitary gland extract can be given in the case of too-weak contractions of the uterus to move the kittens downward and out. This type of injection may be repeated at intervals. It should not be given until the cervix is completely dilated by preliminary labor stages. These weak contractions may go on for some time. If the mother cat's uterus does not respond to this stimulus sufficiently, there is no way for her to get the kittens out. Surgery must be resorted to. Sometimes the head, or the kitten itself, is too large to pass through the pelvis. If help of a professional nature is not given in time, not only will this kitten die, but the others of the litter due to follow must wait too long, their placentas separate from the wall of the uterus, and they die in the uterus for lack of oxygen.

A dead kitten is an immediate source of possible infection to the mother cat. She too may die of this infection, or she may be unable ever to have another litter. If a mother cat has been in labor a long time she may be too weak from pain and effort to survive the anesthetic, if surgery is required. Also, if she has become toxic from the presence of dead kittens in her uterus, she is a poor risk for surgery.

There are two possible solutions to the situation in which the kitten is unable to pass through the opening between the pelvic bones:

1. *Use of Forceps*

An expert veterinarian may remove the kitten, which is probably dead by this time, carefully extracting it, little by little, with forceps. As the mother must be under anesthetic for him to do this, the remaining kittens will have to be removed the same way. They usually will not survive this method of delivery.

2. *Caesarian Section*

A Caesarian section may be performed, and is always indicated, if there is a chance the kittens are alive and if the mother cat is in good condition. Anesthesia is required for either forceps delivery or Caesarian section. However, in the Caesarian operation, there is the additional strain and shock to the mother cat when the uterus is exposed to the air, as is necessary. It is up to the veterinarian to make the decision as to which method is the best for him to use, according to the individual circumstances. His primary concern, and yours, is for the life and well-being of the mother cat.

Except for very unusual circumstances, there can always be another litter of kittens. Many cats have survived several Caesarian sections.

The mother cat who has had an anesthetic during delivery is not herself until twelve to twenty-four hours have passed. Provisions have to be made for the feeding and care of the kittens. If you put the kittens with her before she has completely recovered from the anesthetic, they might hurt her and she might bite them, not realizing fully what is going on. (A side, or flank, incision for Caesarians is the most satisfactory. The mother can lie comfortably on one side and she does not have a sore spot near any nipple.)

The Kitten a Mother Ignores

If your mother cat ignores a new kitten and you can see no reason why, there is probably something internally wrong with the kit which the mother senses. Nature is cruel as well as wonderful. You may hand-feed this rejected kit and keep it going for days, but chances are you'll lose it anyway.

Care of the Kittens

For the first month of life, the new little ones will require no care on your part, except your changing the towel, blanket, or sheet in their box. The mother cat takes care of their toilet needs until they start eating supplementary food, at which time she begins training them to use the litter box. You will want to look at the little ones often, however, and when you are looking at them, it would be wise to inspect them for fleas. All the fleas from their mother will soon transfer to the little helpless kittens.

Sometimes I invert a cardboard box over their bed, making a "den" for the mother and her kits. They seem to like this arrangement. A door is cut in the box, of course, for mother cat to go in and out. Needless to say, the mother cat is fed more often than the usual twice-a-day feeding, as she must now produce sufficient milk to keep the little ones growing. You will find a section in Chapter VIII on feeding kittens.

Kits from six weeks on are most amusing. You have no idea how much fun you will have watching them play. At about eight weeks of age, they start developing their individual personalities, and about this time you will find a "pet" name for each.

Kittens should not be sold before they are at least eight weeks old. Four months is a much better age to sell them, but most people want to buy the youngest kitten they can get. We try to hold all of ours until they are ten to twelve weeks old, anyway. The longer they are with their mother, the stronger they become, and the more ready they are to make the transition to a new home. Of course, you may want to keep them all, but this can become impractical. No doubt you will want to keep one. Then, if you are planning to have the mother altered, she will have company. Remember, two cats are more fun than one. The little guys grow up fast and will be cats before you know it. If you decide to keep a kitten, don't forget to give him his shots. You may want to give all the kittens their shots before they go to new homes, but it is often difficult to get the additional price you must have to pay you back the cost of the shots. People always want to buy pet kittens for as little as possible. If you are having just one litter, you will no doubt have friends waiting to buy your kits. If you plan to continue breeding for litters to pick up a little extra money, don't bother. It just does not work out that way. You soon will realize you are losing money instead of making it.

Drying Up a Mother Cat's Milk

If a queen loses all her kittens, or if for any reason she is suddenly left with milk and no kittens, she will soon become very uncomfortable. Nature will take care of this problem in a few days. Put some olive oil or white vaseline on her breasts. She will no doubt lick it off, but neither of these preparations will harm her. It would be wise to withhold milk from her diet. If a breast becomes infected, it will require treatment by your veterinarian. If you are selling the kittens, try to space the sales so that this particular problem does not have a chance to develop.

CHAPTER XIII

BREEDING

In breeding, we try to produce the most perfect specimen possible. First of all, we are interested in the whole cat, not just a lovely head, but eye color, body structure, coat, balance, and personality. From time to time we are blessed with a cat having exotic beauty of body and movement, particularly when we have bred very carefully with the hope that from the litter would come the show stopper of all time. But we are never satisfied. We keep trying to produce a cat still better and even more striking.

Breeding Goal

Breeders try to improve the breed in accordance with the standards set forth in Chapter II, and they try to produce their interpretation of "The Perfect Siamese Cat." This cat has never been produced, nor will it ever be. But to try is most intriguing. The first step is to read some of the many books devoted entirely to genetics which may be found in your local library. If you purchased your cat from a breeder, that person will be happy to guide you. If you show your cat, you will meet many Siamese breeders at the shows, and from them you will learn much about breeding. Sometimes your information will be contradictory, but here is the essence of breeding: each person develops his own vision of the cat he would like to produce and works out his own techniques and ideas of how to do it. Therefore, evaluate all you read and hear, and experiment for yourself. There is always more to learn.

Inbreeding—Line Breeding—Out-Crossing

Take a good look at the animals you are working with. Study the pedigree of each, but use strong healthy cats for breeding. Inbreeding is a very important tool for the development of desired characteristics, such as head type, eye color, coat texture, body structure, etc. Remember, however, that inbreeding magnifies bad points as well as good ones; therefore, it is not wise to breed cats with obvious or known faults. A question often asked is, "What is the difference between inbreeding and line breeding?" Webster's Dictionary tells us that inbreeding is breeding "by continual mating of individuals of the same or closely related stocks," and that line breeding "is the production of desired characteristics in animals by inbreeding through several successive generations." Therefore, line breeding is simply a form of inbreeding. A breeding of unrelated cats is known as an out-cross. While inbreeding is used to amplify certain existing characteristics, an out-cross is used to obtain whatever characteristics are desired, but lacking. For example:

Cat #1 possesses exceptionally fine head type, but he and all his relatives lack body type, so an out-cross becomes desirable if you are trying to obtain a cat with good head type as well as a good hard, muscular body. Thus, Cat #1 is bred to Cat #2 who has good body type, but not particularly outstanding head type. The result will be Cat #3, who has less head type but better body type than Cat #1, and less body type but better head type than Cat #2. Since both head and body type exist in Cat #3, an inbreeding, such as brother-sister, would amplify the existing chatacteristics. From this mating will result Cat #4 which would be the third generation away from Cats #1 and #2. Cat #4 would very strongly resemble his grandparents, but would probably be better than either.

The foregoing is an example of the "Third Generation Rule," which is very important in obtaining a cat close to your ideal. You will find yourself trying many combinations, some of which will "click" while others will disappoint. Too much inbreeding will produce small, weak, and sickly animals. The point at which you feel an out-cross is wise, and what out-cross to use, is for you to choose.

Don't be surprised to find yourself plotting, figuring, and charting breedings with another member of your family, and spending hours discussing and forming your own theories about breeding. The hard part is waiting for kittens to grow to maturity so you can breed the next stage of your plan, and then waiting again for those kits to arrive, develop, and mature so they, in turn, may be bred. The more you learn, the more interesting and complicated it becomes.

Color Breeding

Some breeders like to work with just one color of Siamese, while others prefer to work with more than one color. Recently, Mr. James Kilborn, of Seattle, Washington, a Siamese breeder and judge, developed the following chart (reprinted from ACFA Bulletin, August, 1962) which is delightfully understandable, with a bit of humor added. If you will study it for a few minutes, you will find you can tell just what color kittens will result when different colors of Siamese are bred together.

Siamese Breeding Chart
Compiled by Jim Kilborn

	1	2	3	4	5	6	7	8	9
1	1	1 2	1 3	1 2 3 4	2	2 4	3	3 4	4	1
2		1 2 2 5	1 3 2 4	1 2 3 4 2 5 4 6	2 5	2 4 5 6	3 4	3 4 4 6	4 6	2
3			1 3 3 7	1 2 3 4 3 4 7 8	2 4	2 4 4 8	3 7	3 4 7 8	4 8	3
4				1 2 3 4 2 5 4 6 3 4 7 8 4 6 8 9	2 4 6	2 4 4 6 6 9	3 7 8	3 4 7 8 8 9	4 6 8	4
5					5	5 6	4	4 6	6	5
6						5 6 6 9	4 8	4 6 8 9	6 9	6
7							7	7 8	8	7
8								7 8 8 9	8 9	8
9									9	9

LEGEND
1. SEAL POINT
2. SEAL POINT WITH BLUE FACTOR
3. SEAL POINT WITH DILUTE FACTOR
4. SEAL POINT WITH BOTH FACTORS
5. BLUE POINT
6. BLUE POINT WITH DILUTE FACTOR
7. CHOCOLATE POINT
8. CHOC. POINT WITH BLUE FACTOR
9. FROST POINT

OFFICIAL SANS* BREEDING CHART
BASED ON EXPERIMENTS CONDUCTED BY AH CHOU

NEUTER	SPAY
0 0	0 0

*SOCIETY FOR ADVANCEMENT OF NEUTERS AND SPAYS

EXAMPLE: IF SIRE IS A BLUE POINT WITH A DILUTE FACTOR AND DAM IS A SEAL POINT WITH A DILUTE FACTOR... LEGEND SHOWS SIRE AS TYPE 6 AND DAM AS TYPE 3... CHART SHOWS RESULTS OF THIS MATING AS 2,4,4,8... THEREFORE, THIS MATING WILL PRODUCE AN AVERAGE OF 1/4 SEAL POINTS WITH BLUE FACTORS, 1/2 SEAL POINTS WITH BOTH FACTORS AND 1/4 CHOCOLATE POINTS WITH BLUE FACTORS.

CHAPTER XIV

CAT ASSOCIATIONS AND CLUBS

Cat Fanciers' Associations

Currently there are six National Cat Associations, a list of which follows, with the name and address of the Secretary on the left and of the Recorder on the right:

THE CAT FANCIERS ASSOCIATION, INC. (CFA)

Mrs. Myrtle Shipe
20615 Patton Court
Detroit 29, Michigan

River Hill Building
Suite 5
39 East Front Street
Red Bank, New Jersey

THE AMERICAN CAT ASSOCIATION, INC. (ACA)

Mrs. Stanley Gibson
Lakeside, Berrien County
Michigan

Mrs. Stanley Gibson
Lakeside, Berrien County
Michigan

AMERICAN CAT FANCIERS ASSOCIATION (ACFA)

Mr. Porter Walley
1104 Bouldin Avenue
Austin 4, Texas

Mrs. Porter Walley
1104 Bouldin Avenue
Austin 4, Texas

THE UNITED CAT FEDERATION, INC. (UCF)

Mrs. Lynne Baker
1311 Loganrita Avenue
Arcadia, California

Mrs. Mary Ann Maxwell
P.O. Box 1067
Spring Valley, California

CAT FANCIERS FEDERATION, INC. (CFF)

Mr. Richard P. Orman
P.O. Box 8763
Philadelphia 4, Pennsylvania

Mrs. Florence Kanoffe
Route 80
North Guilford, Connecticut

NATIONAL CAT FANCIERS ASSOCIATION, INC. (NCFA)

Mrs. Frances Kosierowski
8219 Rosemont Road
Detroit 28, Michigan

Mrs. Frances Kosierowski
8219 Rosemont Road
Detroit 28, Michigan

Every cat club throughout the country is affiliated with one of the above associations. When a club puts on a show, it is sponsored by the club's national affiliate and is governed by the association's rules. Hence, different shows have different rules, and sometimes slightly varying standards for the different breeds of cats. Also, at shows conducted under the rules of the ACFA, UCF, and CFF, you will usually find Havana Brown cats, Rex cats, and Red Point Siamese, whereas, at this writing, the ACA and CFA do not recognize these new breeds.

How to Join a Club

Any breeder you are able to contact in your area should be able to give you information on what clubs are in existence in the area, and whom to contact regarding membership. If you attend a cat show, the officers of the club putting on the show are listed in the front of the show catalog. You could contact any of them regarding membership.

You could write each of the secretaries of the national organizations listed at the beginning of this chapter and ask the name of the secretary of the club nearest to you. If there is no club in your area, you could start one. Any of the national secretaries will be happy to give you information on how to start a new club. If you ask all of the associations for their aims and rules, I am sure they will send them to you. Then you could pick whichever you feel you would like best to become affiliated with. The only reason a national association might not care to have a new club started would be that there already are too many clubs in the immediate area.

The primary purpose of all clubs is to further the welfare of all cats. It is common practice for them to donate regularly to some local cause, as, for example, the Society for the Prevention of Cruelty to Animals. Many clubs invite a speaker, such as a veterinarian or someone well versed in genetics, to give a talk after their business meeting. Each club usually puts on a show once a year or once every two years. Sometimes a club sponsors dinners or programs to raise money for its treasury.

If you are interested in cats, you will enjoy being a member of a club. You will meet others as interested in cats as you are and be able to "talk cats" to your heart's content. Ordinarily, we soon get the feeling we are boring others if we talk about our felines, inasmuch as most people do not share our interest with the same intensity.

Normally, clubs acquire new members by having one of their members invite a prospective member to a meeting as a guest. If the prospective member likes what he sees and indicates a desire to join the club, he is asked for an initiation fee. He is then voted upon at the next meeting of the club. Usually, he is accepted. Newcomers frequently are assigned duties so they

Chocolate Point female owned and bred by Clare L. Scott: DBL. CH. GLORY-S CHOCOLATE REVEL. Sire: Yabour's Mr. Hi-Tone; dam: Chocolate Fudge of Glory-S. Photo by Hans Bomskow.

may become acquainted with the others more quickly and realize they are active and important members of the club. Always at show time there is much work to be done, and, more often than not, not enough members to do it.

A Few Interesting Facts

The latest census on cats indicates some 30,000,000 cats in the United States and Canada. This figure puts the cat population higher than the number of dogs estimated in the same area.

The Cat Fanciers Association registered 150,000 cats in 1962 alone.

CHAPTER XV

SHOWS

How to Obtain an Entry

After you have purchased or bred a fine cat, you just can't wait for a show to come along, but your first problem is to get an entry to the show. Entries usually are sent to people who previously have entered a show in the area. Once on these lists, you have no problem. Entries usually close about a month prior to the show date, so you won't be able to bundle your cat under your arm and take him to the show the day it starts. He must be listed in the catalog.

If you have access to *Cats Magazine*, as I have said elsewhere, you will find listed therein all the coming shows under their heading CAT SHOW CALENDAR, together with the name of the club giving the show, the national association sponsoring it, the judges, whether or not it will be All American scored (explained in Chapter XVI), and the show secretary's name and address. Write the secretary of the show you are interested in and ask to be put on the entry mailing list. If you don't have *Cats Magazine*, ask a breeder in your area to let you know when a show is coming up so you can ask for an entry. Newspapers are not a very good source, because by the time a show is advertised it is only a week or two away, although occasionally a club will place an ad in the local newspaper stating that there is to be a show, that the entries will close on a certain date, and give the name of the person to contact for an entry.

Entry Blanks

When you receive your entry blanks, a sheet or two of information regarding the show will be included, such as the size of the cages and whether or not you will be required to furnish your own litter pan and litter. Almost without exception, exhibitors are asked to furnish their own water and feeding dishes. You will be told whether or not horse meat will be furnished, and how often. Fees for entering will be listed. Every show consists of an All Breed Show, in which every cat must be entered, a Long Hair Specialty Show, and a Short Hair Specialty Show. You will want to enter your Siamese in the

Short Hair Specialty, in addition to the All Breed Show.

The current trend is for two clubs to combine their efforts and give a "double" show. This means there are two All Breed Shows and two, each, of the Long Hair and Short Hair Specialties. Of course, the entry fees double, too, but you are entering your cat in four separate shows, and, if you are lucky, your cat could complete a full championship during a two-day show. The usual fee for a double show is $8.00 to $10.00 per cat. A listing fee is also required for each cat that is not registered in the national association sponsoring the show. This is usually fifty cents for each All Breed Show, or $1.00 for a double show. The exception, as mentioned in Chapter V, is a show sponsored by CFA, as this organization requires every cat entered in championship competition to be registered before being entered. After filling out the entry or entries, return them with the appropriate fees to the entry clerk, who will send you entry confirmation.

Cost of Putting on a Show

Perhaps you are thinking the fee for entering a cat in a show is exorbitant? I would like to point out that it is quite expensive to put on a show, and not every show ends up on the black side of the ledger. The club giving the show must first rent the show hall. The entry blanks and information sheets must be printed and mailed. Usually several hundred of them are sent out, requiring quite a tidy sum for postage alone. Cages must be rented, including judging cages, unless the club owns its cages. Judges must be contracted for and paid approximately $50.00. For a double show, at least four judges are required. The judges' travel, lodging, and food expenses while they are away from home are paid for by the club. Most judges travel by air, as they have jobs to get back to as soon as possible. There are rosettes, ribbons, and trophies to purchase. All this easily could add up to between two and four thousand dollars. Suppose the club gets 250 entries, at $10.00 each. This is $2,500.00. (The catalog should pay its own way with ads which have been sold.) The club hopes that paid admissions will make up the difference plus enough left over to show some profit.

Getting Ready for the Show

If you intend to show your cat, groom him for showing from the time he is a kitten and try to keep him in peak condition at all times.

Of course you have always been feeding him good food, with vitamins, and he is in good condition: his coat shines and lies close to his body. You have not permitted him to be infested with fleas or ear mites, and you have had him wormed when he needed it. You had him inoculated for both pneumonitis and cat fever. (It might be wise to obtain a booster shot for both about a month before the show, as it is likely he will be exposed to them at the show.) You have him well groomed, and his claws clipped. If you have permitted him to become fat, don't even bother to enter. A fat Siamese cat has lost all his beauty and svelteness. On the other hand, I do not mean to imply that you should starve your cat, by any means. He will "go down" for emaciation as fast as for overweight.

Cage Decorations

The information sheet that came with your entry blanks gave the dimensions of the cages. Decorating your cage, or cages, serves several purposes, such as the following:

Cage drapes protect the cat from drafts.

Cage drapes enable you to build your cat a little "cave" where he will feel secure and reasonably happy because you will be there with him (he probably will receive more attention from you during the show than you have time to give him at home).

Cage drapes prevent cats from seeing each other and fighting through the cages.

The manner in which you decorate your cages enables you to show your cat to the public to the best advantage. Use colors that will show him off. If you are artistically inclined, you may go to any length you wish to decorate the cage as attractively as possible. However, if you are practical, like the least amount of work possible, and don't have a lot of time to make fancy

Seal Point female owned and bred by Nellie K. Van Schaik: QUAD. CH. PONTATOC'S VAN ACRES CHANDA. Sire: Ch. Dusadi the Bold Venture; dam: Pontatoc Na-Lee. Photo by Hans Bomskow.

curtains or to do them up after the show, I would suggest using a straight piece of 39" material approximately four yards long—washable, of course. This may be fashioned to fit any size cage. It is sufficient to drape a double cage or it can be folded for a single cage. All shows do not utilize the same size cages.

In addition to the cage curtains, a rug, approximately 24×36 inches, for the bottom of the cage, adds to the appearance. It is nice to have it match or pick up a color in the drapes. Another length of material or a matching towel may be used to go over the top of the cage. A matching pillow to put in the cage not only is attractive to look at but the cat will appreciate it to curl up on while watching the passing parade of spectators or for sleeping. You might like to have a piece of decorative screening to go in front of the litter box to give him some privacy. Incidentally, don't be upset to find that the cat will probably prefer to sleep in the litter box!

A List of Things to Take Along

The evening before the show, it is fun to get out all the things you will need and pack them in a suitcase. Some suggestions for items to include are:

An extra rug for the cage bottom, in case of an accident.

Water and food dishes. Tops of cottage cheese containers are handy for feeding, and they can be thrown away after being used.

A thermos or plastic bottle of your own city's water for the cat, if you are to be away from your own city. A change in water easily upsets a nervous stomach—even your own.

A can opener, and a spoon for dishing food out of cans. Your cat may not like the horsemeat furnished, and you will want to feed him something else. Usually, pet food companies distribute samples during a show, but it is well to have a few cans of your cat's favorite food on hand. Many owners take strained baby meats for their cats to eat at shows, as these do not upset or bloat the cat's stomach.

A roll of paper towels or a box of tissues.

Grooming agents: rubber brush, flea comb, and chamois.

Pen or pencils to mark your catalog with (or perhaps to write a letter).

Some small pliable wire and a wire cutter. Usually, you will have to wire your cage in places to be sure the cat can't poke his way out of it when you're not looking.

A paper sack for refuse.

Disinfectant and sponge with container for water to wash the cage before decorating it.

Ash tray (bean bag type preferable) and matches.

Blanket and pillow. *You* may wish to "cat nap" in your car.

Comfortable shoes.

Show Time

You get up early, as this is finally the big day. I suggest you feed your cat a light meal while you are dressing to give him time to use his litter box before he is popped into his carrier. Excitement is not conducive to good digestion.

When you first arrive at the show, you will be required to stand in line with your cat until the veterinarian checks him and admits him. Just before you get to the veterinarian, you will receive an envelope with your cat's number on a card, and an exhibitor's ribbon for you to wear. The veterinarian checks every cat for signs of illness, ear mites, and ringworm. When he finds your cat to be well and healthy, he initials the cat's card, and you go on into the show room and find your cat's cage.

When you have found the cage, wash it thoroughly inside and out with disinfectant. Some people use alcohol. The reason for washing the cage is that you don't know what animal was in it last or what infection or disease it may have had. Germs of all kinds could be on it. Besides, it is probably just plain dirty. Your cat will rub up against the front of the cage many times during the show, and if he gets a smudge on his coat, believe me, it will defy removal—at least until after the show is over. You may take the cage off the table and set it on the floor to wash and decorate it, if you wish. It is easier to get at it when on the floor. After it is washed, swing the top back in place, secure it, then lift it by the top to see if any gaps appear that a cat could push his way through. If so, take a piece of the wire you have brought along and wire it closed, being careful not to leave any sharp ends protruding for the cat to hurt himself on. Before replacing the cage on the table, place the rug.

Decorate the cage as you had planned. Many prefer to put the cage curtains inside the cage, but too often the cat is found between the curtains and the cage, exchanging snarls with another cat in an adjacent cage, both cats becoming quite upset. A cat does not show to advantage if he must be "dug" out of this situation just before it is time to take him up for judging. For this reason, I like to drape my cages on the outside. I have found that safety pins are best to fasten curtains to the bottom of the cage. I like to use clips for the top fasteners. Sometimes drapery hooks are used, but a cat could easily hurt himself on these trying to get out of the cage. You may note, when you have time to look at other cage decorations, that the cages containing Persian cats are very elaborately decorated with fancy beds, dressers, vases, and many frills. Siamese are much too active for all of this, and would have it torn up before you could turn around.

When the cage is decorated, set it in place and add the litter box and litter, the cat's water dish, and his pillow. It is a good idea to take a disposable litter box along to the show, as sometimes the show's source of supply doesn't deliver in time or doesn't deliver enough of them.

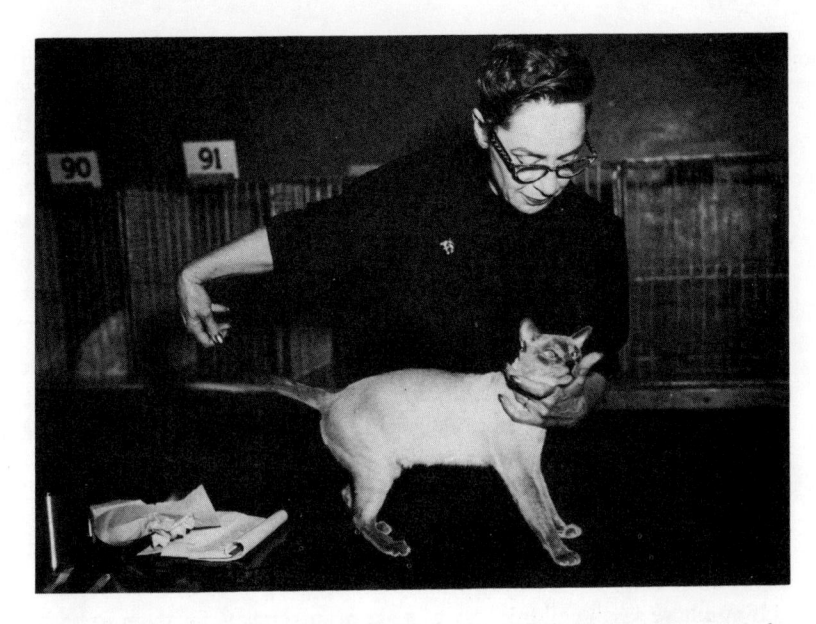

Judge Lavona Wright demonstrates part of the technique used for judging the fine points of a Siamese at a show. Photo by Louise Van der Meid.

It is wise to put a big safety pin around the clasp on the cage door. I have seen mischievous children running down the aisles, occasionally stopping to tweak open a cage when they thought no one was watching. Another thing children and adults visiting a show do is stick their fingers in each cage as they go along looking at the cats. First of all, they run the risk of being bitten. A cat who is not used to the show circuit may be very frightened.

Another important aspect is that these people could be spreading disease from one cat to another. For this reason, you will see many exhibitors put a sheet of clear plastic in front of their cages. It is wise to have on hand some of this plastic, obtainable at almost any variety store, to put in front of your cages when there is a crowd and you have to leave the area. It is also well to have some in case the show room is cold. It is not uncommon to see a cat in a fancy coat or knitted sweater when the room is cold.

Leaving the Cat Overnight

Most shows last two days, and if you have traveled several hundred miles to the show you will be staying at a motel or hotel overnight. You will want to take your cat with you. However, if you are staying with friends or you have several cats at the show, you may not be able to do so. If you know you will be leaving a cat in the show hall overnight, take a blanket along with which to cover the entire cage. Before you leave, push the cage back as far as possible from the edge of the table and place a folding chair on top of the cage to be sure the cat can't push the cage off the table and get out. There is no more horrible feeling than to return to the show hall next morning and find your cage empty—but this happens frequently. Most exhibitors take their cats with them for the night, if it is at all possible.

Show Etiquette

The first rule: never feed anyone else's cat without the owner's permission. You might be accused of doing so to keep the cat from winning. A Siamese cat is never fed before he is judged. If he were, his stomach might pouch out and cause him to appear fat.

It is considered a courtesy to the judge to have the cat's claws clipped.

Don't take your cat to the show if he is coming down with something. It is not courteous to other exhibitors to expose their cats to whatever yours might be getting. Besides, you will be endangering your own cat's health.

If you have small children, try to make arrangements for them to be cared for at home. Small children running through the show room are very distracting to the cats, the judges, other exhibitors, and to you. Children become bored and tired as the long hours drag on.

A can of spray deodorant (non-injurious to cats) comes in handy to counteract unpleasant odors. Odor-absorbing products are available at your pet store.

It is wise to have some first aid items on hand for your own use as well as to help others, should the occasion arise. Such items would be aspirin, Band-aids, cotton swabs, antibiotic ointment, and Aqueous Zephiran (no colored antiseptics).

You will see many cages decorated with ribbons and rosettes won at previous shows: these must be displayed inside the cage, whereas wins made by a cat at the current show are hung on the outside of the front of his cage.

"Cat out!" This phrase called out loudly strikes terror to the heart of every exhibitor. All doors are barred immediately. No one is allowed in or out until the cat is located. Everyone is instructed via loud speaker to stand still and remain quiet to permit the owner to locate and secure the cat. Then it is announced that the cat has been caught, and the show goes on.

The Show Circuit

Showing your cat is a great game and can be a lot of fun, especially if you are able to take in distant shows as well as local ones. You soon make your own circle of friends and you learn a great deal about human nature as well as about raising, breeding, and showing cats. You learn to be a good loser and a gracious winner.

If a friend's cat becomes lost, you feel as bad as he does, and you do your utmost to help find the cat.

Showing often involves a long drive on a Friday night after work to arrive just in time for a show Saturday morning. On Sunday night, usually very late, when you are tearing down your cages and packing up to start the long trek home, a friend nearby will ask, "Are you going to the show next weekend?" That show may be nearly a thousand miles away, but your answer will probably be yes! The next week-end arrives and all of you are at this distant show. If the show management is inexperienced, you pitch in and help them put the show on. Perhaps you get so busy you don't have time to take your own cats up to be judged, and a friend will realize the situation and signal from across the room that he will take the cat up for you.

Maybe you are lucky and had enough money to fly to this show. Of course the trip both ways is enjoyable, and you get your sleep for a change because you are home so fast you get to bed at the usual time. Usually, though, you will be driving through the night and will have much time to reflect on all facets of the show. Maybe you are pondering about how it is possible to be feeling so depressed on Saturday night, yet be floating on "Cloud Nine" all the way home (this being if you made some nice big wins).

Agenting Cats

Sometimes people will agent cats. If a friend or acquaintance can't attend an out-of-town show, yet wants his cat shown, you may be asked to show the cat for him. This is a responsibility for which the usual fee is $10.00, or more, depending on how great a distance the cat must be taken. If you are agenting a cat, you take exactly the same care of him as you do of your own. If you are asking someone to agent your cat, be sure you ask a person you know will take as good care of him as you do yourself, plus showing him to his best advantage.

Jungle Cats on Display

Shows often have various jungle cats on display. Most of us who love Siamese cats would like to own one of these exotic creatures. The first obstacle is the high cost of importation. The most popular of the jungle cats is the ocelot, very beautiful, lovable, and intriguing.

CHAPTER XVI

SHOW COMPETITION AND NATIONAL SCORING SYSTEMS

Show Competition

Kittens

Any kitten from the age of four to eight months may be shown in the kitten class. All kittens of the same color and sex of Siamese are compared together, and the best male and best female of each color are chosen. These two kittens are then compared, and the better of the two is given the Best of Color (BOC) ribbon. The other kit is given the Best of Color Opposite Sex (BOX) ribbon. This comparison progresses through each color of Siamese. Then the BOC and the BOX winners are compared and a Best Siamese Kitten and a Best Siamese Kitten Opposite Sex are named. After all the kittens in the show have been judged, the "bests" of each breed are compared together, and finally, a Best Kitten and Best Kitten Opposite Sex are chosen, and each of these kits is awarded a rosette, and a trophy if it has been donated for the win. Kittens do not compete for championships.

Adult Competition

An unaltered cat shown for the first time as an adult (past his eight-month birth date) is shown in the "Novice" class.

If he wins a first, or winner's, ribbon (depending on which association's rules are governing the show), he must be shown in the "Open" class at the next show he attends given by the same association. For example:

All the male Blue Point Siamese novices are compared and the best one is given a first ribbon. Then all the male Blue Point open cats are compared, and the best is given a first ribbon. The two cats with the first ribbons are then compared, and the best of the two is given a "winner's" ribbon. This ribbon carries with it the championship points of the show. Usually three of these winner's ribbons are required for a championship, except by CFA and ACA, where four are required. Then all male Blue Point champions are compared and the best is given a first ribbon. The male with the winner's ribbon is compared with the first-ribbon cat in the champion class, and the best of these two is chosen. This cat is the best Blue Point male in that particular show.

The female Blue Points are judged in the same manner, and a best female is chosen. The best male and the best female Blue Point are compared, and the best of these two is determined. This one is given the BOC ribbon, and the other is given the BOX ribbon.

The "Champion" class is for cats that have completed the championship requirements in the association sponsoring the show and have confirmation of the championship.

The "Grand Champion" class is for cats that have completed the required number of wins to qualify for Grand Champion in the association sponsoring the show, and have been so confirmed. Different associations require a different number of Grand Champion points to qualify. Some associations require fifteen Grand points while others require twenty. A cat receives a Grand Champion point for a certain number of Grand Champions defeated. If there are Grand Champions competing in a class, the cat winning the first ribbon in this category is compared with the cat having received the winner's ribbon and the one having received the first in the Champion class, and from these three, the best male or female is picked and given the BOC or BOX ribbon.

This same comparison and choosing goes on through the males and females of all the other colors of Siamese in the show. When all have been judged, the judge picks a Best Siamese from the four (or five, it is an ACFA show) cats who have received the BOC ribbon, and Best Siamese Opposite Sex from those cats which have received the BOC or BOX ribbons. The show then progresses and all cats in every color of every breed are judged and a Best and Best Opposite Sex is chosen for each color, and from these a Best of Breed and Best of Breed Opposite Sex are chosen.

When it comes time to do the show finals, a Best Domestic Short Hair and Opposite Sex are picked and a best Foreign Short Hair and Opposite Sex. From these four cats, a Best Short Hair and Best Short Hair Opposite Sex are chosen. Best Novice and Opposite Sex, Best Open and Opposite Sex, Best Champion and Opposite Sex, and Best Grand Champion and Opposite Sex are chosen. Finally, a Best Cat in Show, Best Cat Opposite Sex, Second Best Cat and Second Best Opposite Sex are picked from the previous winners. Each of these wins is given a rosette, and many are given trophies.

In a Short Hair Specialty Show, only the Domestic and Foreign Short Hairs compete, so the cats winning Best Short Hair and Opposite Sex are also the Best Cat in Show, and Best Cat Opposite Sex.

In an All Breed Show, a Best Long Hair and Best Opposite Sex Long Hair are picked, and the Novice, Open, Champion, and Grand Champion bests are picked from both the long- and short-haired cats. The Best Cat and Second Best Cat and their Opposites also are picked from all cats eligible.

Some associations require that the judge pick a Reserve winner, and some give ribbons for the Reserve wins. The purpose of a Reserve win is that if the winner is disqualified for any reason, the win goes to the Reserve winner. In like manner, if the Best Cat is disqualified for any reason, the Second Best Cat gets the win. The cat winning Second Best Cat may or may not also be named Best Cat Opposite Sex.

Neuter and Spay Competition (Premier or Peerless)

People who own altered cats can enter their cats in shows. There is a special class for the altered cats. Some associations call them "Premiers"; one calls them "Peerless." These cats win championships within their own competition the same way as described under Novice-Open competition for adult cats. The best altered cat and opposite is picked in the same manner as in the unaltered classes.

ACFA Shows

Shows sponsored by this association differ in a number of ways from other shows. Every cat in the adult championship classes is given a score slip on which the judge marks off for various things, and this score is included on the posted judges' slips, also, along with the winners of first, second, third, and possibly fourth, Best of Color and Best of Color Opposite Sex.

Another difference is that the Championship classes are divided into Junior and Senior Champions, and the cats with the first ribbons in each of these two classes are compared and a Champion Winner's ribbon is awarded. The cats with the winner's ribbon, champion winner's ribbon, and grand champion first ribbon then are compared to determine the best male or female of a color class. In this association, cats win double, triple, and quadruple championships. When they win the fifth championship in an ACFA show, they are eligible for confirmation as a grand champion, provided they have won scores of 95 or more under seven different judges for which they are confirmed Royal Merit, and have won a three "Final" wins under three different judges. They then may go on to double and triple Grand Championships by building up Grand Championship points. Thirty Grand Championship points are required for each additional Grand Championship. These Grand points are acquired by defeating Grand Champions and extra Grand points are given for certain "Final" wins.

This association also recognizes wins made in other associations, enabling a cat to build up his multiple championships. A recent ruling requires that a cat win his first championship in an ACFA show, after which his owner may claim credit for wins made in other associations by applying to the secretary of the ACFA and paying a fee of 50c. for each such win claimed.

Grand Championship—Except in ACFA

In all other associations, after a cat becomes a champion, he wins grand championship points by defeating three or four other champions for each grand championship point, depending on the association. Certain wins such as Best Cat carry with them additional grand championship points. Usually, a cat may build up only four grand championship points in each individual show. Two associations permit a cat to accumulate five grand championship points per show. Long before you will need to know these fine points, you will have the latest rules of each association which specifically spell out its individual requirements.

"Points" of a Show

The points toward championship that a cat wins when he is awarded the red-white-and-blue winner's ribbon (purple winner's ribbon in CFF) are measured by the number of adult cats competing in the championship classes. All CFA shows are four-point shows, regardless of the number of cats competing. The show rules usually included with your entries list the number of cats required for two-point, three-point and four-point shows. One association, UCF, conducts five-point shows. The cost of putting on a show these days practically precludes the possibility of there being less than enough cats competing to make the show a four-point show. In other words, if sufficient entries are not received to pay for the show's expenses, the show is usually cancelled. Occasionally you may find a show management that is carefully counting the absentees to determine if there are enough "counters" competing to be able to announce to the exhibitors that the show is a four-point show. Cats competing in Kitten, Household Pet, Any Other Color, and Neuter and Spay classifications are not considered counters. Only unaltered adults competing in championship competition are counters.

Different associations require a different number of points for championship. Some require ten, others require twelve, some require sixteen. For example, suppose you are attending a double show, and your cat will be shown under four different judges. Suppose the cat is able to win the "winner's" ribbon on all four sides, and the show is a four-point show. He will have won sixteen points toward championship. However, the association sponsoring the show may require only ten championship points to qualify for champion. Your cat would be a champion, and you would simply drop the extra six points. If the show is sponsored by ACFA, the fourth winner's ribbon would count on the cat's second championship, and would not be lost.

Championship Confirmation

As soon as your cat completes a championship, you should write the recorder of the association in which the cat has qualified, asking for confirmation of the championship. There is usually a fee of $1.00 for this confirmation. Some associations require that you register your cat with them within a certain length of time after you have won a winner's ribbon. Others require that you register the cat within a certain length of time after the cat has qualified for champion. All associations require a cat to be registered with them before the cat can be confirmed a champion and compete in the championship class. Read your show rules carefully for each association, and watch these time limits. As mentioned in Chapter V, a cat cannot compete in a CFA*show as an adult until it is registered with CFA. A safe rule to avoid losing credits won in the other associations is to register the cat in the association as soon as it wins a "winner's" ribbon in that association.

Titles

The proud owner of a cat that is a triple champion in ACFA will not hesitate to state that the cat is a triple champion. If this owner would qualify his statement and say the cat is a triple champion in ACFA, the statement not only would be clearer, it would be more correct. This may become quite confusing. General usage dictates that a cat using the title of triple champion actually be a champion in three different associations. If a cat has Double Grand and Quadruple Champion in front of his name, it means he is a Grand Champion in two associations and a champion in four. However, since a cat may win multiple grand championships in ACFA, and must accumulate 30 Grand Championship points to do so and be in the finals to qualify, if he is a Double Grand Champion in ACFA and a Grand Champion in another association, he is entitled to use Triple Grand Champion in front of his name.

A cat is usually listed with his full combined title in advertisements and in places such as the photographs in this book. However, when being entered in a show, he should be listed only with the title he has won in the particular association sponsoring the show.

National Scoring Systems

Cats Magazine—All American Scoring

All wins are scored automatically by the All American scorer for *Cats Magazine*, if the show is to be All American scored. In order to have a show so scored, the club putting on the show must clear the show dates with *Cats Magazine* and pay a fee to have the show scored. A club should contact the editor of *Cats Magazine* for the exact fee required. Beginning with the 1963-64 show season, *Cats Magazine* scores only one show per weekend in each of its four sections of the country.

If you are interested in exactly how your cat is scored, write to *Cats Magazine* and ask for a reprint of their All American scoring rules. This will enable you to count up the points your cat wins, and you will be able to keep track of your competition, too. If you feel your cat is eligible for a sectional win, it is wise to list his wins with the scores you have determined and send it to the All American scorer in March of each year. This scoring consists of two parts:

Color Points

A cat in adult competition is given one point for every cat in his own color

* See footnote page 65.

class, including himself, when he wins Best of Color.

A cat that wins Best of Color Opposite Sex is entitled to one point for every cat in his own color class of the same sex, including himself.

Class Points

Only adult cats count up class points. Count the class points on the highest win your cat makes. For example: if a cat is named Best Siamese and Best Short Hair Opposite Sex, add up a point for each Siamese class and a point for each class of his own sex in the rest of the Short Hair classes. Don't count the Siamese classes twice. If these awards were won in an All Breed show and the cat also wins Best Champion Opposite Sex, he is entitled also to a point for each champion class of the same sex in the whole show. Don't give him a point for each champion class of his sex in the Short Hair Divisions, as you have already given him these points when you added his score for Best Short Hair Opposite Sex.

If a cat won Best Short Hair and went on to win Best Cat in Show in an All Breed show, he would be entitled to a point for every class in the show. Don't bother to count the classes in the Short Hair Division. Start from the beginning of the adult championship competition and count a point for each class in which there was at least one cat present. Of course, you would not count the classes in the Household Pet, Any Other Color, Neuter and Spay or Kitten competition.

In any one show, a cat has won the total of his Color and Class points.

Second Best Cat Award Differs in Counting

This win is counted by adding every class in the show and multiplying it by .85 (85%). Second Best Cat Opposite Sex does not count for anything. If a cat wins both Second Best Cat and Best Cat Opposite Sex, he is entitled to a full point for every class in the show of his own sex and 85% of the classes of the other sex.

When a Cat Cannot Claim All His Points

No cat may be given credit for more points than the total won by the Best Cat in Show, less one point. It is possible for a cat having won one of the top wins to come out with more points than the Best Cat. The Siamese color classes are sometimes very large, while the Best Cat may be in a class by himself. If this happens (with a Second Best Cat win usually), the cat having won more points than Best Cat in Show is entitled only to the number of points the Best Cat won, less one.

Kitten Counters

Kitten counters differ in that only the awards of Best Kitten and Best Kitten Opposite Sex count. Color and class points are not involved. A kitten having been awarded Best Kitten is entitled to a point for every kitten present and competing. If a male kitten wins Best Kitten Opposite Sex, he is entitled to a point for every male kitten in the show, including himself.

Sectional Awards

The sections in *Cats Magazine* awards are Western, Midwestern, Eastern, and Southern. Each year *Cats Magazine* names its sectional winners in its August issue. The cat making the highest score by the above method in each color of each breed, male and female, is named, for instance, All Southern Seal Point Female. This would be abbreviated AS. The cat making the second highest score in each color of each breed, male and female, is named Western Honorable Mention Chocolate Point Male, for example, abbreviated WHM, or AWHM.

Kitten and Neuter and Spay Sectional Awards are given to the Best Shorthair male and female, Honorable Mention Shorthair male and female, Best Longhair male and female, and best Longhair Honorable Mention male and female only.

All American Awards

In each year's September issue *Cats Magazine* names the highest scoring cat, male and female, of each color of each breed, from the section winners together with the honorable mention winners. They also name the cat, male and female, who is highest scoring of each breed. The highest scoring and honorable mention male and female Long Hair and Short Hair are named. The ten top All-American cats are listed with their scores. The highest awards named by *Cats Magzine* are Cat of the Year and Opposite Sex Cat of the Year.

All American and All American Honorable Mention awards are listed for only the Best Shorthair male and female and best Longhair male and female for both kittens and Neuters and Spays. Also, Kitten of the Year and Opposite Sex and Premier or Peerless and Opposite are named.

Certificates, Ribbons and Rosettes Awarded

Each sectional, All American, and honorable mention win is awarded an attractive certificate suitable for framing, together with a ribbon awarded by *Cats Magazine* for each sectional and honorable mention win. The All American and honorable mention wins are awarded rosettes.

Cats Magazine Award Abbreviations

In explanation of the abbreviations commonly used in connection with show awards the following are examples:

AW 60 means All Western, show season closing in the spring of 1960 (actually the show season of 1959-60, beginning in the fall of 1959).
AHM 59 means American Honorable Mention, 1959.
HM, means Honorable Mention (second highest scoring).
AM, AA 59 means All Midwestern and All American, 1959.
AS, AHM 56 means All Southern and American Honorable Mention, 1956.
HSAW means All Western and Highest Scoring cat in the Western Section.

ACFA Merit Awards

This Association has a national scoring system of its own, called Annual Merit Awards. You can win in this competition as well as in the All American competition. Since each ACFA show gives individual score slips to each cat in championship competition, each cat's scores are averaged at the end of the season, and the highest and second highest score in each color and breed, male and female for each of their regions of the country are named, as well as the highest and second highest scoring cats in each color and breed, male and female, for the whole United States and Canada, called Inter-American and Inter-American Honorable Mention. All of these awards are published annually in their August bulletin. Each regional winner is sent a ribbon, and rosettes are sent to the kittens.

The regions of ACFA are Northern, Northeastern, North Central, Northwestern, Southeastern, South Central, and Southwestern.

A cat must have at least nine scores to average. If a cat has ten to fourteen scores to average, the lowest score may be dropped. If a cat has fifteen or more scores to average, the two lowest may be dropped before his average score is computed. Thus, if a judge gives the cat a low score, when all the rest of the judges who have scored him during the show year have scored him high, the low score need not pull down his overall average, as was the case in the past.

ACFA has recently given kitten awards, also. Since kittens aren't scored in their shows, a kitten is given credit for each kitten in the show that he defeats, and the Best Kitten Opposite Sex is given credit for each kitten of his own sex he defeats. The Short Hair male and female kittens and Long Hair male and female kittens for each region are named in the August Parade of Royalty, together with the Best Kitten and Opposite Sex of all Regions.

Some Regional and Inter-American Abbreviations

In the ACFA Parade of Royalty and in some of the photographs in this book you will find abbreviations designating ACFA regional and Inter-American Awards, as follows:

Royal NC means North Central Region, and cat has qualified for Royal Merit title, sometimes abbreviated RM.

Royal SW means Southwestern, Royal Merit.

Royal SC means South Central, Royal Merit.

Royal HM Inter-American means honorable mention (second highest scoring) in the United States and Canada, or in all of the regions.

SIAMESE LORE

BY SALLY LEE CROWDER

My cat owns me, as you may see.
His name is Nai Mana Lee.
He is a prince of old Siam;
Blue Point, with pedigree, Pek-Le-Tam,
Recorded in DiNapoli's plan;
Aristocrat, as all his clan.
The jewels which adorn his eyes
Are sapphires, shining with surprise
When scolded for his impish desire
(Inherited from his lordly sire).
To rendezvous with things so high,
Sometimes I think he'll jump to the sky.
He struts, his tail a question mark,
"Where is the softest seat to park?"
He reads my script with silent gaze.
If thoughts were words, he would amaze.
Serene and gorgeous, undisturbed—
I wish I were as unperturbed!

Nearly five years ago, Nai Mana Lee was purchased from me. A copy of the poem reproduced here was sent me while this book was in process of publication, and I decided to include it as an example of one owner's sincere expression of feeling for her pet.

Nai Mana Lee has another mistress now, for recently Sally Lee Crowder passed away suddenly. I found a new home for him, where he has a Blue Point just his age to share his new mistress's high fourposter.

Now and then she holds him close and murmurs in his ear—for the mistress he won't see for a while.

INDEX

A

ACA (see *American Cat Association*)
ACFA (see *American Cat Fanciers Association*)
ACFA Bulletin, 215
Agents for cats, 227
Albino Siamese,
    history of, 23
    personality of, 38
Albumen, 130
All-Pets Magazine, 46, 190
Altering
    advisability of, 54
American Cat Association, 65, 217
American Cat Fanciers Association, 217
Ammon Ra's Taisho, 9
Anemia, 157
Aqueous Zephiran, 226
Arsenic, 147
Arthur, Noel, 9
Arthur, Mrs. Helen, 9
Aspirin, 157
Associations and clubs
    how to join, 218
    list of, 217
    officers of, 217
Asthma, cats' relation to, 108-9
Awards
    abbreviations for, 234
    ACFA Merit, 235
    All American, 234
    Cat of the Year, 8
    certificates, 234
    Opposite Sex Cat of the Year, 8
    regional, 235
    sectional, 234

B

Baba Kiti, 23
Baker, Mrs. E. T., 9
Baker, Mrs. Lynne, 217
Bathing, 114-5
Birds
    killing of, 28-9

Birth
    breech, 202
    trouble during, 211-2
Bites, 153
Blackheads, 179
Blow-flies, 149
Blue-Creampoint Siamese, 23
Blue Point
    personality of, 36
Body
    color, standard for, 16
    type, standard for, 15
Bond, Dorothy, 112
Boren, Carlon, 8
Breech birth, 202
Breeding
    for color, 215-6
    goals, 214
    types of, 214-215
Burton, Lilly A., 23

C

Caesarian, 139, 212
Cage decorations, 222
Cages
    cleanliness of, 185
    for one cat, 185
Calcium, 126, 198
"Calling," 194-195
Carbolic acid, 147
Carriers, 92-93
Cat Fanciers Association, 45, 65, 217, 219
Cat Fanciers Association Year Books, 8
Cat Fanciers Federation, 217
Cat fever (see *Feline enteritis*)
Cats Magazine, 8, 46, 190, 220, 232-235
Cattery
    ideal, 182-183
    names, 58-59
    registration of, 185-186
CFA (see *Cat Fanciers Association*)
CFF (see *Cat Fanciers Federation*)

Chetham-Strode, Warren, 32
Chlordane, 146
Chocolate Point
    personality of, 36
Circulation, 203-204
Claws
    care of, 115-116
Cleft palate, 209-210
Clothing for cats, 109
Coat
    grooming, 113
    Standard for, 16
Coccidiosis, 164
Cod liver oil, 126
Cold, simple, 158
Colors
    Any Other Color, 23
    Blue Points, 18
    Chocolate Points, 18
    Lilac (Frost) Points, 21-22
    Red (Red Colorprints)
        Points, 22
    Seal Points, 18
    Standard for, 18-23
Condition
    Standard for, 18
Constipation, 146
Convulsion, 158
Coryza, 175
Curiosity, 39
Cymri Dee-Va, 9
Cystitis, 155-157

D

Dangers
    from appliances, 101-105
    from aspirin, 157
    from Christmas trees, 100
    from foods, 134
    from House Plants, 99
    from poisons, 146-148
    from shoulder-riding, 101
    from wool, 108
DDT, 146
De-clawing, 120-122
Diarrhea, 145
Diet, 128-134
Double mating, 196
Dulce Domum's El Coco of
    DiNapoli, 59

E

Ears
    care of, 116
    Standard for, 12
Ear mites, 165
Eclampsia, 198
Eczema, 150
Egg yolk, 130
Euthanasia, 210
Eye color
    Standard for, 13
Eye shape,
    Standard for, 13
Eyes
    care of, 116-118
    open at birth, 210

F

Fat in diet, 128-130
Feeding
    amount of, 132-133
    method, 133-134
Feline distemper (see *Feline enteritis*)
Feline enteritis, 168
Flattened rib cage, 210
Fleas, 118-120
    danger from, 119
    removal of, 119-120
Frost Point (see *Lilac Point*)

G

Galvin, Peggy, 111
Gibson, Mrs. Stanley, 217
Gingivitis, 179
Gould, Owen, 8
Grooming, 113-122

H

Hairballs, 177-179
Havana Brown, 218
Head
    Standard for, 10-11
Heat, 195
Hecht, Mrs. R. H., 8-9
History, 8
Hydrogen peroxide, 148

I

Illingsworth, Esther, 112
Income taxes, 186
Infectious feline panleucopenia, 168

Intestinal abnormalities, 209

J

Johnstowne, Mrs. Lucy C., 8
Journal of the American Veterinary Medical Association, 157
Jungle cats, 227

K

Kanoffe, Mrs. Florence, 217
Kilborn, James, 215
Kittens
    abnormal, 209
    birth of, 200-202
    care of normal, 212-213
    care of premature, 206
    feeding of, 123-126
    how to choose, 49-57
    how to find, 46
    nest for, 205
    price of, 50-53
    registration of, 63-65
    usual number of, 205
Kosierowski, Mrs. Frances, 217

L

Lanolin, 108
Larson, E. John, D.V.M., 157
Layton, Barbara, 112
Legs and feet
    Standard for, 15
Lilac (Frost Point) personality, 36
Lindane, 146
Liquid medication, 141
Lockehaven Siam, 8
Longevity of cat, 66
Lungs, removing fluid from, 203

M

Madison California, 8
Maggots, 149-150
Magner, Lillian, 9
Maxwell, Mrs. Mary Ann, 217
Meats in diet, 128-131
Milk
    aversion to, 28
    in diet, 130-131
    mother's (drying up), 213
    soy bean, 176
Miscarriage, 198-200

N

Names of cats
    length of, 59-61
    pet, 58
National Cat Fanciers Association, 217
NCFA (see *National Cat Fanciers Association*)
Neck
    Standard for, 15

O

Objection (in Standard), 10-23
Opposite Sex Cat of the Year, 8
Origin of Siamese cat, 7
Orman, Richard P., 217

P

Parasites, 158-166
Pedulla, Lillian, 9
Personality
    variance by color, 35-38
Phenol, 147, 157
Pills, 139-141
Placenta, 202-204
Pneumonitis, 170-176
Points (color)
    Standard for, 18
Points (scoring)
    class, 233
    color, 232
    for kittens, 233
    Second Best Cat, 233
    when not allowed, 237
Poisons, 146-148
Pregnancy
    duration of, 197
    feeding during, 198
    symptoms of, 198
Purchase of Siamese, 44-57

Q

Queen, visiting, 192-195

R

Rabies, 166
Red Colorpoints (see *Red Points*)
Red Points (Red Colorpoints)
    personality of, 38
Registration
    of cattery, 185-186
    papers, 45

Respiratory infections, 170-176
Rex, 218
Rhinitis, 175
Ringworm, 148-149
Rodin's Sun Ling, 23
"Rolling," 194
Roundworms, 161-163

S

Scoring systems, 228-235
Scratching post, 77-80
Seal Point
 personality of, 35
Seams and stitching, 40-42
Season, 195
Sexual behavior in male, 187
Shipe, Mrs. Myrtle, 217
Shipping, 94-95
Show competition
 awards for, 228-235
 for adults, 228-230
 for kittens, 228
 for neuters and spays, 230
 types of, 228-235
Show calendar, 46, 220
Shows
 cost of, 221
 entry blank for, 220
 equipment needed at, 223
 etiquette for, 226-227
 preparation for, 223
Sickness, symptoms of, 136-139
Sleeping habits, 105-107
Spraying, 187-188
Standard, show, 10-23
Stud cat
 definition of, 188
 fee, 190-192
 how to locate, 188-190
Stud tail, 179
Surgery, 139

T

Table scraps, 132
Tail
 Standard for, 15
Ta-Lee-Ho's Al-La-Bi, 8
Tapeworm, 119, 160-161
Teeth
 care of, 118
 treatment of sore, 118

Temperature
 how to take, 144
 normal, 144
Tempurra's Yours Turly, 8
Thiamin, 134
Ticks, 166
Tortiepoint Siamese, 23
Toys, 81-83
Training
 need for gentleness in, 66-71
 to a whistle, 87
 to bathtub, 87
 to car and boat, 89-90
 to leash, 75-77
 to litter box, 83-84
 to retrieve, 81
 to sit up, 88
 to stay indoors, 72
 to toilet, 84
Translations from the Siamese, 32

U

UCF (see *United Cat Federation*)
United Cat Federation, 217
Uremic poisoning, 155

V

Vaccinations (see *Viral diseases*)
Vee Roi's Katisha, 9
Vee Roi's Lantara Gene, 8-9
Veterinarian, choosing, 135
Viral diseases, 166-176
Vitamin A, 126
Vitamin B, 128, 157
Vitamin B1, 134
Vitamin C, 179
Vitamin D, 126, 198
Vitamin E, 134
Vitamins
 for mother cat, 198
 need for, 126-128
Voice, 32

W

Walley, Porter, 217
Walley, Mrs. Porter, 217
Watch cats, 39-40
Water in diet, 131
Wolfgang Liebsti II of Thani, 9
Wolfgang's Melody of Be-Ba, 9

Y

Yellow fat disease, 134